NOVA SCOTIA
BOOK OF
Everything

Everything you wanted to know about
Nova Scotia and were going to ask anyway

John MacIntyre ▪ Martha Walls

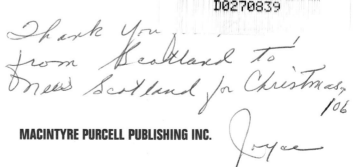

To: David

Thank You...
from Scotland to
new Scotland for Christmas,
106

MACINTYRE PURCELL PUBLISHING INC.

Joyce

MacIntyre and Purcell Publishing Inc.
1662-#332
Lunenburg, Nova Scotia
B0J 2C0
(902) 482-3152
www.johnwmacintyre.com

Cover photo courtesy of Nova Scotia Department of Tourism, Culture and Heritage.
Cover and Design: Channel Communications Inc.

Printed and bound in Canada by UGS.

Library and Archives Canada Cataloguing in Publication
MacIntyre, John,
Walls, Martha,
Nova Scotia Book of Everything / John MacIntyre, Martha
Walls.
ISBN 0-9738063-0-3
1. Nova Scotia--Miscellanea. I. II. Title.
FC2311.M335 2005   971.6

Introduction

No book can be a book about everything, of course. Not even the venerable Encyclopedia Britannica can make that boast. What we've tried to do with *The Nova Scotia Book of Everything* is give you information that you should know; information that you might like to know; and lastly, information that is downright fun.

From the best greasy spoons, to five of the scariest criminals, to the best beaches, it is all here. We tell you how much we earn, how much we drink, and how many of us live rural versus urban. When we started this project, we had one guiding principle and that was to deliver a book that would be interesting, entertaining and useful.

The rule of thumb was that if it was interesting to us, it makes it in; if it doesn't, well, it sits on the sidelines. The problem we ran into was that time and space meant that there was plenty of stuff we would have liked to have included, but simply couldn't. Next time.

Putting together a book of this type inevitably is a product of a team of people. Wynne Jordan, Holly Gordon and Nick Hatt helped and participated in the writing and research of the material. Elva and Judy Purcell pored over the final manuscript looking for inaccuracies or inconsistencies. Then there are the people who supplied us with the things they love, find peculiar, or just find downright interesting about Nova Scotia. They took time out of busy schedules, and we think you'll be glad they did. At any rate, we had a lot of fun putting this book together. We hope you have as much fun reading it.

John MacIntyre, Martha Walls, September 2005.

Table of Contents

INTRODUCTION 3

FAREWELL TO NOVA SCOTIA 7

TIMELINE 9
From 10,000 BC To 2005 . . . Joseph Howe . . .Thomas Raddall

NOVA SCOTIA ESSENTIALS 19
From the Official Flower to Origin of Bluenoser to the Largest Towns
And Cities. . . .Halifax, Capital City . . . Those Unusual Place Names
(Hello Ecum Secum)

SCOTIA SLANG 35
From Come-From-Away to Double-Double. A Primer on Nova Scotia
English . . .Thomas Haliburton . . .Haliburtonisms

GEOGRAPHY 45
From Kilometers of Coastline to Highest Mountains. . . .Those Bay of
Fundy Tides . . . Sable Island . . . Michael Haynes's Five Favourite
Hikes . . .Silver Donald Cameron's Five Favourite Beaches

WEATHER 55
Highs, Lows, Record Rainfalls, and Hurricane Juan . . . .
Peter Coade's Five Weather Phenomena . . . Five Foggiest
Towns . . . Les Suetes.

POLITICS 67
From The Treaty of Paris to Pre And Post Confederation . . . A
Premier Primer . . .Profile Of Angus L. . . .Dr. Murray Beck's Five Most
Important Political Figures . . . Premier John Hamm's Five Favourite
Nova Scotians Throughout History.

THEN AND NOW 77
Wages, The Horseless Carriage, Electric Power . . . The Halifax
Explosion . . . Lunenburg . . . Bluenose Remains Undefeated.

ECONOMY 87

From GDP to Debt, Taxes, Wages . . .Five Most Common Jobs . . . Top
Five Things Nova Scotia Households Spend Their Money On . . . Top
Five Exports . . . Profile of Jodrey . . . Sobey . . . Alexander Keith . .
.Bluefin Gold.

CRIME AND PUNISHMENT 109

From the First Murder to Public Hangings in The Halifax Commons .
. .Slave Trade . . . Prohibition and Rum Running . . . Donald
Marshall, Jr. . . . Dean Jobb's Five Most Devious Criminals. . .
Expulsion of the Acadians.

FIRST PEOPLES 127

Mi'kmaq Culture, Medicinal Cures, Invention . . .Place Names . . .
Games . . . Myths . . . Political Structure . . . Treaties . . . Rita Joe . . .
Daniel Paul's Five Important Nova Scotia Mi'kmaq.

BLACK AND WHITE 143

A Tale of Two Races . . . Slavery . . . Shelburne's Unkept Promise . . .
Sierra Leone . . . Africville . . . Kirk Johnson

TAKE FIVE 155

Ashley Macisaac's Five Favourite Nova Scotians . . . Michael Haynes
Five Favourite Greasy Spoons . . . Sue Macleod's Five Favourite
Fictional Characters . . . Joel Plaskett's Five Favourite Halifax Hang-
Outs . . . Anne Simpson's Five Phrases That Describe Nova Scotia . . .
Ecology Action Center's Five Environmental Achievements . . . Tim
Tregunno's (Halifax Seed) Five Hardiest Nova Scotia Flowers . . . Harv
Stewart's Top Five Current Nova Scotia Sporting Figures . . . Trudy
Fong's Five Favourite Nova Scotia Backroads . . . Bruce Nunn's Five
Surprising Nova Scotian Connections To The World . . . Nancy
Stevens' Five Favourite Nova Scotia Landscapes . . . Marjorie Willison's
Five Favourite Plants . . . Colleen Jones' Five Favourite Sporting
Activities . . . Allan Lynch's Five Favourite Places . . . Muriel
Duckworth's Five Inspirational Nova Scotia Women . . . . . Alain
Meuse's Five Favourite Fish Stories.

Farewell To Nova Scotia

"Farewell to Nova Scotia" is the unofficial anthem for the province. It is a sailor's lament of unknown authorship. It is believed to have been written during or just before the First World War and is thought to have been derived from "The Soldier's Adieu" attributed to Scottish poet, Robert Tannahill. It was discovered by celebrated Nova Scotian folklorist Helen Creighton.

The sun was setting in the west,
The birds were singing on every tree.
All nature seemed inclined for to rest
But still there was no rest for me.

Chorus
Farewell to Nova Scotia, you sea-bound coast,
Let your mountains dark and dreary be.
For when I am far away on the briny ocean tossed
Will you ever heave a sigh and a wish for me?

I grieve to leave my native land,
I grieve to leave my comrades all.
And my parents whom I held so dear
And the bonnie, bonnie lassie that I do adore.

The drums they do beat and the wars do alarm,
The captain calls, we must obey.
So farewell, farewell to Nova Scotia's charms
For it's early in the morning I am far, far away.

I have three brothers and they are at rest,
Their arms are folded on their breast.
But a poor simple sailor just like me
Must be tossed and driven on the dark blue sea.

Nova Scotia:

A Timeline

10,000 BC - 1497: An estimated 12,000 to 75,000 Mi'kmaq live in Mi'kma'ki, their territory consisting of the eastern half of the Gaspe, New Brunswick, Prince Edward Island, Newfoundland, mainland Nova Scotia and Cape Breton Island.

June 1497: Giovanni Cobatto (John Cabot) lands on Nova Scotia, and whets European appetites with tales of the massive cod stocks of the North American coast.

1524: The term "**Acadie**" is first used by an Italian explorer Giovanni da Verrazano, to designate a large region of northeastern North America.

1605: First French Settlement is established in Nova Scotia at Port Royal, near present day Annapolis Royal.

1606-1607: The first social club in North America is established; the *Order of Good Cheer*, which encourages regular merriment and feasting, is established to help settlers at Port Royal pass cold, lean, winter months.

1610: Mi'kmaq Grand Chief Membertou is baptised by Jesuit missionaries, becoming the first Catholic convert in Nova Scotia.

1613-1763: Nova Scotia is a North American battleground in a series of wars and skirmishes between France, England and the Mi'kmaq.

1632: Three hundred French settlers, the first "Acadians," establish a thriving French colony in Nova Scotia.

1713: France establishes Fortress of Louisbourg, a truly a multi-cultural fortified community on the edge of the continent, at Cape Breton.

1749: Halifax established by Britain to counter French Louisbourg.

1752: North America's first newspaper, the Halifax Gazette, is established.

1755: Eleven thousand Acadians (about 75 percent of all Acadians) are expelled, sent around the globe by Britain, when Acadian loyalty comes into question after 300 Acadians are found defending the French Fort Beauséjour. Acadians refuse to take an unqualified oath of allegiance to Britain.

1758: Fortress Louisbourg falls for the second and final time to England, marking the beginning of British rule in Nova Scotia.

1740s-1750s: Responding to Britain's desire to populate Nova Scotia with Protestant Europeans, more than 2000 "foreign Protestants," German and Swiss colonists settle in Nova Scotia, at present-day Lunenburg.

1759-1774: "Planters," Yankee settlers with farming predilections, are enticed to Nova Scotia, promised free religion and freer land.

Bio JOSEPH HOWE

Joseph Howe was born in Halifax in 1804 to a humble Loyalist family engaged in the printing trade. By the age of 13, Howe and his oldest brother joined the family printing business. At the age of 24, Howe purchased the most important colonial newspaper, *The Nova Scotian*. It was a decision that would change his life and the life of his province forever.

Always interested in politics, in 1835 Howe's paper published a letter critical of the fiscal abuses of the local government and alleged that £30,000 was "taken from the pockets of the people." At the time, the publishing of such an incendiary article was susceptible to charges of criminal libel, and Howe was inevitably charged and stood trial. Taking the stand in his own defense, Howe delivered to the court a six-hour rousing speech in which he not only spoke in his own defense, but in defense of the very principle of freedom of the press.

People's Choice

Riding high on his public popularity after winning the case, Howe was elected to the Nova Scotia House of Assembly the next year. He was soon made leader of the Liberal party and set about ushering in a series of government reforms, known collectively as Howe's "12 Resolutions." The reforms essentially tempered the power of aristocratic, colonial politicians, transferring some of it to the people.

In 1848, thanks to Howe's leadership, Nova Scotia became the first British colony to achieve responsible government. Less successful was Howe's anti-confederation campaign. Staunchly opposed to union with Canada, Howe feared that it would undermine a grander British Empire. He also opposed confederation on practical terms. With eerie foresight, he believed that the terms of union would crush the economy of Nova Scotia.

Howe, however, could stave off neither his political opponent, Charles Tupper, nor the push to union. The year after the 1867 union, Howe continued to oppose it and fought in vain for repeal. With the cause lost, Howe was eventually persuaded to go to Ottawa to join in the building of the new country.

1773: The famed ship Hector lands at Pictou, bringing 189 Scottish settlers to "New Scotland."

1770s-1780s: The "Great Awakening" stirs Nova Scotia when Henry Alline, a young Nova Scotian with a flare for the dramatic, preaches his evangelical message to throngs of excitement starved Nova Scotians, stirring a Christian revival in the fledgling colony and establishing here the roots of a strong Baptist tradition.

1775-1783: When the American Revolution erupts in 1775, Nova Scotia's transplanted Yankees bring great relief to British officials when they do not support their rebelling homeland, but opt instead to become the "neutral Yankees."

1783: When 30,000 colonists loyal to the British Crown are forced to flee the 13 colonies, a diverse group of 19,000 Loyalists settle in Nova Scotia, creating a massive logistics headache for colonial officials, and hardship for the Acadians and Natives told to "shove off" to make way for the Loyalists.

1784: Nova Scotia is partitioned into three colonies: Nova Scotia, New Brunswick, and Cape Breton.

1820: Cape Breton loses its independent colonial status and (reluctantly) rejoins Nova Scotia.

1848: Nova Scotia becomes the first British colony to get responsible government.

1850-1880: Nova Scotians prosper, engaged in the shipbuilding and shipping industry in this, the "golden age" of sail.

1864: Although Nova Scotian delegates attend the Charlottetown Conference prepared to consider "Maritime Union," no deal could be reached. The meetings conclude with a proposal for Confederation which is hammered out a month later in Quebec. Anti-Confederates, led by Joseph Howe strongly opposed the "Quebec resolutions" while pro-Confederate Charles Tupper called for their adoption.

July 1st, 1867: Nova Scotia becomes part of Canadian confederation but "better terms" is the rallying cry of disaffected Nova Scotians who felt forced into Confederation.

1892-1894: Nova Scotia-born John Thompson is Canada's fourth Prime Minister.

1914-1918: As World War One rages, almost 3,500 Nova Scotians and Prince Edward Islanders (the provinces dead are grouped together by the Department of Veteran Affairs) pay the ultimate price.

December 6th, 1917: Two munitions ships, the Mont Blanc and the Imo, collide in Halifax Harbour, catch fire and explode, detonating 2,653,115 kg of explosives in the most powerful non-atomic, man-made blast in history. Almost 2,000 Haligonians are killed and property damage is estimated at $35 million (or $430 million in today's currency).

1918: Women in Nova Scotia get the right to vote provincially and federally.

March 26th, 1921: The original Bluenose is launched from a wharf in Lunenburg. The ship sinks off of Haiti in 1946.

1937: The Canadian Mint first emblazons the Canadian dime with the Bluenose image.

Bio THOMAS H. RADDALL

Born in England in 1903, Thomas Raddall Jr. came to Canada in 1913 after his father accepted a military posting to Halifax. In the final months of WW1, his father was killed in action, essentially leaving a very young Thomas as the only male figure in the house. It was an obligation that would shape his life and writings.

As a 16-year-old, he secured a job in the Canadian Merchant Marine, staying there for three years before taking a job as a wireless operator on Sable Island. The lure of a permanent job back on the mainland brought him to Liverpool, where he worked as the accountant for pulp and paper mills on the Mersey River.

If aspiring writers complain of their lot today, they would be wise to read Raddall's autobiography to see just how difficult it was for Raddall to earn a living from the trade. Throughout his career, he never received a single writer's grant, and by the time the province recognized what they had in their midst (they offered him the Lieutenant Governorship), he and his writing belonged to the country and the world.

Amazed Nova Scotians

Raddall's early writings were short stories and were picked up by major mainstream magazines in the U.K. and the U.S., which of course had the concomitant effect of launching his career in his own country. What amazed Nova Scotians was that a writer of Raddall's ability could see in them stories worthy of telling; more amazing still was that that there was an appetite on the part of the public to read them.

Raddall's 1939 short story collection, The Pied Piper of Dipper

Creek, garnered immediate popular and literary success – winning for him the Governor General's Award for Literature. A string of books followed, each centered on significant events in the history of his province.

The Nymph and the Lamp

Nova Scotia during the American Revolution was at the heart of His Majesty's Yankees, a book that was followed by *Roger Sudden*, an account of the fall of Louisbourg. In 1948, Raddall's non-fiction masterpiece, *Halifax: Warden of the North*, a history of Halifax, became the second of Raddall's works to win the Governor General's Award. His most highly regarded book was The Nymph and the Lamp, which drew upon his experiences as a radio operator on Sable Island.

In total, Raddall won three Governor General Awards in a very productive writing career. In total, he wrote more than 20 books and 32 radio and TV scripts. In 1968, Raddall retired from writing, keen to do so before his writing ability deteriorated with age.

Once asked, "Aren't you afraid of running out of material down there in a little town on the Nova Scotia coast? Why don't you move up to Toronto where there are all kinds of people and where there are all kinds of things going on?" Raddall replied, "When I run out of material where I am, I'll let you know." He never did.

Thomas Raddall died in Nova Scotia in April 1994.

1939-45: Almost 60,000 Nova Scotia men enlist in the Canadian armed forces, and 2525 would die in battle.

December 10th, 1954: Nova Scotia is permanently connected to Cape Breton Island with the completion of the Canso Causeway.

July 1957: Twenty-two scientists from ten nations converge on Pugwash, Nova Scotia to discuss nuclear disarmament, establishing the "Pugwash Conferences" as ongoing international meetings aimed at "reducing the danger of armed conflict and seeking cooperative solutions for global problems."

October 23rd, 1958: The Number Four mine at the Cumberland Rail & Coal Co. in Springhill, Nova Scotia experiences a "bump," trapping 174 men 13,000 feet underground for eight days, while the world watched. Tragically, 75 miners are killed.

1962: Nova Scotia mall rats rejoice as the province becomes home to the Halifax Shopping Center, North America's second air-conditioned shopping mall.

1983: Prince Charles and his wife Princess Diana of Wales, newly a mother to the heir to the throne of England, visit Nova Scotia.

September 1984: Pope John Paul II visits Nova Scotia.

May 9th, 1992: At 5:18 AM, the Westray coal mine explodes, killing 26 miners.

June 15th - 17th, 1995: The G7 Summit, featuring G7 leaders and a wobbly Boris Yeltsin, is held in Halifax.

September 2nd, 1998: En route from New York City to Geneva, Switzerland, Swiss Air Flight 111 plunges into the Atlantic off Nova Scotia, killing all 215 passengers and 14 crew members.

September 11th, 2001: When terrorists attack the United States, North American air space is closed. Forty diverted planes land at Halifax International Airport. Nova Scotians open their homes and hearts to over 7000 stranded passengers.

Summer 2004: Acadians from around the world gather in Nova Scotia to celebrate the arrival of the first French settlers in Canada four hundred years earlier.

Nova Scotia Essentials

Origin of Name: Latin for "New Scotland." In 1621, Kings James I of England (James VI of Scotland) claimed the land as a part of the kingdom of Scotland.

License Plate: "Canada's Ocean Playground" was adopted on the Nova Scotia license plate in 1972.

Bluenosers: There is a great deal of debate about exactly why Nova Scotians are called Bluenosers. Some say it's because the sailors' mittens were blue and the dye got on their noses when they rubbed them; others, because Nova Scotians' noses turned blue from the cold. And one story has it that the nickname was given to the crewmen of schooners that carried blue-skinned Nova Scotia potatoes to New England in the late 1700s. Regardless of the origin, the term is not derisive. Indeed, Nova Scotia's most famous schooner was called the Bluenose.

Motto: Munit Haec et Altera Vincit (One defends and the other conquers).

They said it

Provincial Flag: The province's flag is the flag of Scotland with the colours reversed. The "Arms" (the lion rampant) in the center of the flag is a symbol of the crown. Nova Scotia is the first overseas British colony to receive its own flag

Provincial Flower: Nova Scotia was the first province to adopt a flower. The mayflower, named because it blooms in May, was official-ly designated in 1901. The mayflower is a spicy-smelling pale pink/white flower that grows in clusters on a shrub.

Tartan: The blue and white in the tartan stand for the sea; the green represents the forests; red for the royal lion on the shield of arms; and gold for the royal charter of the province.

Provincial Bird: The osprey was designated the official bird of Nova Scotia in 1994. There are 250 active osprey nests in the province.

Provincial Dog: Nova Scotia's official dog, the Duck Tolling Retriever, is native to Yarmouth County. Also known as the Little River Duck Dog, the Toller was recognized as a pure breed by the Canadian Kennel Club in 1945.

Provincial Berry: The blueberry was officially designated our provincial berry in 1996. Nova Scotia is Canada's top producer of blueberries. The town of Oxford calls itself the Blueberry Capital of Canada.

Provincial Tree: The most common tree species in Nova Scotia, the red spruce, became the province's official tree in 1998. It grows to a height of 25 metres and its average lifespan can reach 400 years.

Time Zone: Atlantic

System of measurement: metric

Voting Age: 18

Statutory Holidays: Nova Scotia has five official statutory holidays — New Year's Day, Good Friday, Canada Day, Labour Day, and Christmas Day. Most employers also recognize Victoria Day, Thanksgiving, Remembrance Day, Boxing Day, and the first Monday in August.

Never on Sunday: Nova Scotia is the only province in Canada not to allow Sunday shopping.

Capital City: Halifax

Take 5 **TOP FIVE LARGEST**
CITIES AND TOWNS

1. **Halifax Regional Municipality** - population 379,770
2. **Cape Breton Regional Municipality** - 109,330
3. **Truro** - 11,457
4. **Amherst** – 9,470
5. **New Glasgow** – 9,432

AMALGAMATION

During the 1990s, the provincial government developed a strategy for municipal restructuring that created large regional governments out of the smaller municipalities of Halifax and Sydney and their environs. In 1995, the Cape Breton Regional Municipality (CBRM) was formed through an amalgamation of eight former municipalities, boards, and agencies within the County of Cape Breton. The following year, the cities of Halifax and Dartmouth, the town of Bedford and the Halifax County Municipality were combined to create the Halifax Regional Municipality (HRM).

NOVA SCOTIA'S POPULATION: THEN AND NOW

- 1784: 32,000
- 1851: 276,854
- 1901: 459,500
- 1951: 642,600
- 2005: 937,538

POPULATION IN PERSPECTIVE

Nova Scotia is more than twice the size of Massachusetts but there are seven times more people in Massachusetts than here. As a percentage of the Canadian populace, the population of both Nova Scotia and Atlantic Canada has been decreasing for more than 60 years as native Nova Scotians leave the province to look for better opportunities and other provinces attract more immigrants. Nova Scotia today accounts for just three percent of the Canadian population.

Did you know...

That Nova Scotia was once a part of the county of Edinburgh, Scotland? In 1621, Sir William Alexander, wanting to claim the province as part of his territory, declared it part of his barony of Edinburgh.

NOT IN THE MILLION CLUB

Although Nova Scotia's population continues to increase, it is increasing at a decreasing rate. If current birth and out-migration patterns continue, the province is not expected to break the million-people barrier. By 2007, the number of deaths in the province is expected to outnumber births. By 2018, after peaking at 949,000, the population is predicted to begin decreasing.

POPULATION DENSITY

- Tokyo: 13,416 people per square kilometre
- New York City: 10,194.2 people/km2
- Nova Scotia: 17.8 people/km2

BOYS AND GIRLS

- Median age: women: 38.2 men: 38.6
- Life expectancy: women: 81.4 men: 76

- Fertility rate (number of children a woman will have during her lifetime): 1.37

Take 5 TOP FIVE BABY NAMES
IN NOVA SCOTIA

Boys:	Girls:
1. Ethan	1. Emma
2. Ryan	2. Madison
3. Liam	3. Emily
4. Alexander	4. Hannah
5. Noah	5. Abigail

Warden of the North

In 1749, 37-year-old Edward Cornwallis brought an estimated 2,500 English men and women, mostly Londoners, to this rocky, untouched land. Cornwallis was shrewd enough to name his new settlement in honour of his patron, George Dunk, Earl of Halifax and chief lord of trade and plantations. What Cornwallis seemed less concerned about was whether his new settlers had enough time to put together suitable digs to make it through a Canadian winter.

They didn't, and it is estimated that upwards of 1,000 of them perished trying to stay warm and keep dissolute soldiers at bay. Cornwallis ended his days in the warmth of Gibraltar. The new settlers, the ones that made it through that mad winter, must have surprised even themselves when in the spring that followed they began to carve out the beginnings of a community from the forested hillside.

By 1828, when Nova Scotia's most famous patriot, Joseph Howe, was purchasing the Halifax newspaper that would make him famous, Halifax's population had ballooned to 14,500, 1,800 of whom were members of the garrison. It was the center of its own universe, and if it looked anywhere for some party to acknowledge its growing importance it was to London.

This contemporary description of Halifax in 1828 is offered by British soldier, Captain William Moorson, in his book Letters from Nova Scotia:

". . . the wharfs are crowded with vessels of all kinds discharging their cargoes or taking in the returns. Signals are constantly flying at the citadel for vessels coming in; merchants are running about, in anticipation of their freights; officers of the garrison are seen striding down with a determined pace . . . and ladies, tripping along on the tiptoe of expectation . . . "

This was the Halifax Moorson and Howe wished to see. Halifax was a determined upstart wanting to do the Empire proud. There was, of course, another Halifax, just like there was another London, one that Dickens would capture so brilliantly. There was, indeed, enterprise and opportunity in Halifax, but there was also poverty and squalor of Dickensian proportions. On a single street, Albermarle Street of the 1850s, there were more than a hundred rum shops, and upwards of 600 women engaged in prostitution.

Oh Canada

When Canada came calling in 1867, Howe and the majority of Nova Scotians wanted no part of it. Howe envisioned greatness for his little city and province, and that greatness was not going to be achieved by going to Ottawa. In 1867, Howe made the long steam to London one last time.

He was convinced that he could prevail upon Westminster to scrap its plans for the new country they were about to create. In the end, what Howe witnessed first hand was the passage of the Constitution Act without a murmur of debate. To add insult to injury, the legislation that followed — a bill dealing with untended dogs on London's streets — stirred British passions more than the creation of a new country of which he was now inextricably bound.

Apart from interludes during the war years, Halifax has not pulsed with the same mercantile optimism since the 1870s. The merchants and the hustlers have been replaced by the professional classes. Doctors, lawyers, teachers, and especially bureaucrats, have come to succeed them.

Halifax, of course, is no longer a colonial town. The vestiges of the Empire are in the buildings and parks and gardens. The people here have created their own culture and it is a thriving one. The city has a uniqueness and a delightful rough and bawdy edge that has given it a character that anybody spending time here will come to recognize.

CENTURY CLUB

Some of them attribute it to the sea air; others, to simply minding their own business. Whatever the cause, Nova Scotia has a population of people over the age of 100 that is seven times the world average. On the southwestern coast of Nova Scotia that jumps even higher, to 17 times the world average.

Researchers looking into the phenomenon have noticed that Nova Scotians often speak about very aged relatives, and one researcher even noted that there seems to be an obituary of a centenarian in the newspaper at least once every five or six weeks.

In the end, researchers suspect the combination of an active lifestyle, healthy eating and good genetics plays a role in Nova Scotians living to a great old age. The high population of centenarians along the South Shore may also be attributable to the limited genetic make up of the area. This region is still largely descended from German immigrants who settled the area in the mid-eighteenth century, maintaining the propensity to long life within the local gene pool.

THE MARRYING KIND

The average age of first marriage in Nova Scotia is 27 for brides and 28.9 years of age for grooms. Compare that to 30 years ago, when the ages were 21.1 years for women and 23.1 years for men.

FAMILY STRUCTURE

- Percentage of children living in married two-parent households: 75
- Living in common law, two-parent families: 6.2
- Female lone-parent families: 16.4
- Male lone-parent families: 2.4

D-I-V-O-R-C-E

- Divorce rate (per 100,000) in Nova Scotia: 28.2
- Divorce rate in Canada: 36.1

AGE STRUCTURE
- Percentage of population that is under 25: 30.5
- Age 25 - 44: 29 percent
- Age 45 - 65: 26.5 percent
- Age 65+: 14 percent

ON A TYPICAL DAY IN NOVA SCOTIA . . .
- 24 children are born
- 22 people die
- 13 marriages take place, four in civil ceremonies and nine by religious clergy
- 6 people divorce

RELIGIOUS AFFILIATION
Roman Catholicism is the largest religious denomination in Nova Scotia, but the combined Protestant denominations outnumber Catholics.
- Percentage of Nova Scotians who are Protestant: 49
- Roman Catholic: 37
- Muslim: 0.4
- Jewish: 0.2
- Hindu: 0.1
- Buddhist: 0.2
- Of no religious affiliation: 12

LANGUAGES SPOKEN
- Percentage of Nova Scotians whose mother tongue is English: 93.2
- French: 3.8
- Arabic: 0.5
- Mi'kmaq: 0.4
- German: 0.3
- Percentage who are bilingual (English and French): 10.1

PLACE NAMES

The names of places provide us with clues about a history that often remains unknown or is merely speculated upon by visitors or even by its own residents. What the origins of a name reveal can be a place in time, a geographical feature (often lost because of development), or the importance of the naming people. What they've provided Nova Scotians with is a rich treasure of colourful historical markers.

Amherst, Cumberland County: A Mi'kmaq name for it was Nemcheboogwek, meaning "going up rising ground." The town's first name was Les Planches, given by an Acadian settlement in 1672. The French put the village to the torch in 1755. In 1759, the town was given its current name in honour of Lord Jeffrey Amherst, who captured Louisbourg in 1758 in co-operation with Admiral Boscawen.

Annapolis Royal, Annapolis County: This place had two Mi'kmaq names: Esunuskek, meaning "hard ground and well swarded," and Eisuneskwek, meaning "Eison's place." After the basin's discovery by the French in 1604, it took on the name Port Royal. It was later changed to Annapolis after Queen Anne when the fort was captured by the English in 1710.

Baddeck, Victoria County: A derivation of the Mi'kmaq name Abadak or Abadek, meaning two completely different things: a portion of food set aside for someone or a sultry place.

Bedford, Halifax County: First called Sackville, this city was later named in honour of John Russell, the fourth Duke of Bedford (1710-

Did you know...

That Nova Scotia is the sixth province/territory in Canada, and the first in Atlantic Canada, to legalize same-sex marriage.

1771). He was First Lord of the Admiralty and was Secretary of State for the colonies during the founding of Halifax. Before the 20th century, people also called Bedford the "Ten-Mile House," because it was ten miles from an Inn where stage coaches stopped to change horses and where sleighing parties from the city came for entertainment.

Chegoggin, Yarmouth County: This comes from a Mi'kmaq word that meant "great encampment." Another meaning, Isagoggin, means "the place for weirs."

Chezzetcook, Halifax County: A variation of the Mi'kmaq name Chesetkook or Sesetkook. These words mean "flowing rapidly in many channels." The name may have also come from the French saying, chez les coques, meaning "home of the sea birds."

Cogmagun, Hants County: An English take on the Mi'kmaq word Kogumegunuk or Kookemagun, which is said to mean "the crooked river."

Dartmouth, Halifax County: The Mi'kmaq name was Boonamoogwaddy, meaning "Tomcod ground." There are two possible explanations for the English name. First is that it could have been given in honour of William Legge, Earl of Dartmouth, Colonial Secretary from 1772-75. The other, and the more probable of the two, is that it was named for the Devonshire port of Dartmouth.

Did you know...

That the first reported quintuplets in Canada were born at Little Egypt, Pictou County in 1880? The three girls and two boys all died within two days.

Digby: The Mi'kmaq name for this settlement was Oositookun, meaning "an ear." The first English name for it was Conway, given in 1766 by English settlers from Brandywine in New England and a group that moved from Annapolis. The current name was decided by a large group of Loyalists in 1783 that arrived from New England. The name is in honour of Admiral Robert Digby.

Ecum Secum, Halifax County: This name has been in the making since 1809. The word used that year was Ekemsagen, while an 1813 variation was Ekemsikam. By 1845, the well-known "Ecum Secum" spelling was used. The Mi'kmaq name for it was Megwasaagunk or Agwasaagunk, meaning "a red house" or "a red bank."

Garden of Eden, Pictou County: William MacDonald, one of the first settlers around the year 1830, named this place after the biblical garden because of its intense beauty. It is located on the Moose River, on the north side of Eden Lake.

Halifax: The Mi'kmaq name for Nova Scotia's capital was Chebookt, meaning "Chief Harbour" or "Great Long Harbour." The English name was in honour of George Montagu Dunk, second Earl of Halifax and president of the Board of Trade and Plantations at the time.

Kentville, Kings County: This English name was given in honour of the Duke of Kent in 1826, who had visited the settlement in 1794. The Mi'kmaq name was Penooek, meaning "Pineo's Place."

Did you know...

That the highest number of Nova Scotian births in one year occurred in 1961, when 19,624 children were born.

Lunenburg, Lunenburg County: One of two original Mi'kmaq names was Aseedik, meaning "place of clams." The second was Merliguesene, meaning "milky bay." The current town was established in 1753 and named in honour of the Duke of Braunschweig-Luneburg who was crowned King of England in 1727.

New Minas, Kings County: This settlement received its original name, Les Mines, after French explorers found veins of copper at what they named Cap d'Or on the north side of the basin. Les Mines was changed to Minas.

Necum Teuch, Halifax County: It is said that this name probably means "soft sand place," from the Mi'kmaq name Noogoomkeak.

Nuttby, Colchester County: The name's origin is broken into two parts – "Nutt" is part of the family name, McNutt, and "by" means a dwelling or town. Put them together and you get: a dwelling place of the McNutt family!

Nyanza, Victoria County: Named after Lake Nyanza in Africa. A Mi'kmaq reservation existed in this town in the early 1900's.

Parrsboro, Cumberland County: This English version was named after John Parr, Governor of Nova Scotia from 1782 to 1791. The Mi'kmaq word for this place is Awokum, meaning a portage or short-cut.

Pubnico, Yarmouth County: From the original Mi'kmaq word, Pogomkook, meaning "land from which the trees have been removed to fit it for cultivation."

Pugwash, Cumberland County: This name originates from the Mi'kmaq word Pagwechk or Pagwesk, meaning "shallow water or shoal." It was once called Waterford.

Sackville, Halifax County: The Mi'kmaq name for this place was Aloosoolawakade, meaning "place of measles" after a measles epidemic that killed many. The English name come from Fort Sackville, a military fort started at the head of the Bedford Basin by Captain John Goreham in September 1749 for the protection of Halifax. It is believed that the fort's name came from the Viscount Sackville.

Shinimicas Bridge, Cumberland County: This place name, also spelled as Shinimecas, is a Mi'kmaq name meaning "shining river." It is a community located on the Shinimicas River.

Shubenacadie, Hants County: This place name comes from the Mi'kmaq word Segubunakade meaning "place where ground nuts grow."

Stewiacke, Colchester County: Originated from the Mi'kmaq word Esiktaweak, meaning "it oozed slowly out from still water."

Sydney, Cape Breton County: The Mi'kmaq name for Sydney Harbour was Cibou, meaning river or inlet. The city went through many name changes before it acquired its current one. On Denys' map of 1672, Sydney Harbour is written as "La R. Denys." It was known as Spanish Bay before the end of the 17th century. It was called Dartmouth Harbour in Holland's description of Cape Breton Island. The present name comes from Hon. Thomas Townsend, first Viscount Sydney.

Tatamagouche, Colchester County: This name evolved from the original Mi'kmaq word Takamegoochk, which means "barred across the entrance with sand."

Did you know...

That every 40 days in Nova Scotia a marriage takes place in which both parties are teenagers.

Truro, Colchester County: Named after Truro in Cornwall, England, remembered for the surrender of Lord Hopton's troops to General Fairfax after the battle of Naseby. The original Mi'kmaq name was Wagobagitzk, meaning "the bay runs far up," or "the end of the waters flow." This name was in reference to the Fundy tides. The French Acadians called it Cobequid, a name that came from the Mi'kmaq word for the same place.

Washabuck Centre, Victoria County: This name is said to be Mi'kmaq for "an angle of land formed between a river and a lake." There are two other spellings for it — Washabuckt and Astchbuckt. Another name for it is Wosobachuk, meaning "placid water."

Wolfville, Kings County: The Mi'kmaq name for this place was Mtaban, meaning "mud-cat-fish ground." It was first called Mud Creek by the Planters, and in 1829 the prominence of the DeWolf family brought about the current name.

Windsor, Hants County: The Mi'kmaq name for the region was Pesaquid, meaning "junction of waters" referring to the Avon and St. Croix rivers, which flow into the Bay of Fundy. When the French settled the area in 1685 they kept the name. Permanent British settlement began in 1749, when the town was given the name of Windsor.

Yarmouth, Yarmouth County: The area's Mi'kmaq name was Kespoogwit, meaning "land's end," and Yarmouth's name was Maligeak, meaning "crooked every which way." This description referred to the Yarmouth River. Champlain called the place Port Fourchu, "Forked Harbour." This name still applies to Cape Fourchu, on the western side of the harbour. The English name was in use about 1759.

Scotia Slang:
A Dictionary of Nova Scotian English

Every country and region of the world has its own distinct language. Words and expressions have been nurtured and given meaning over time. They inform the jokes we tell and provide us with a shorthand that can only come to be known by living here. Nova Scotia is blessed with a richness of language that can vary from county to county, and of which we can only offer a small sampling here.

Africadia: The term coined by poet, author and black activist, George Elliott Clarke, for Nova Scotia to reflect the social, cultural and economic presence of black people in Nova Scotia, both past and present.

'Antis': Nova Scotians who opposed Confederation.

Bass River Chair: A chair made by the Dominion Chair Company at Bass River, Nova Scotia.

Bluenosers: Slang term for Nova Scotians.

Boston States: New England, a region with which Nova Scotians have traditionally had extremely close ties.

Bud/Buddy: A friend, a pal.

Ceilidh: Common to Cape Breton, these are informal social gatherings featuring Scottish/Irish dancing, music and story-telling.

Caper: Someone from Cape Breton.

Cheticamp Hookers: Not what you think. These are upstanding Acadian women (and men) who live in Cheticamp, Cape Breton and are known world-wide for their rug-hooking skills.

Come-From-Away: Someone from anywhere but Nova Scotia, especially from outside the Maritimes. (CFA for short.)

Dome, The: The most famous drinking establishment in the province, the Liquor Dome, found in downtown Halifax.

Donair: Something akin to a gyro, this sandwich wrapped in pita bread features spicy meat, tomatoes, onions, and a distinctly Nova Scotian sauce which is sweet, creamy and garlicky.

Double-Double: A coffee prepared with two cream and two sugar (see also triple-triple).

Duck Toller: In full, the Nova Scotian Duck Tolling Retriever, a dog bred in Nova Scotia in the early 19th century to "toll," or lure, and retrieve waterfowl.

Dulse: Dried seaweed, enjoyed as a salty snack.

"Dumb as a Stump": Stupid.

"Eh": A truly Canadian phrase, but in Nova Scotia it has an implicit question mark and means "what ?"

Elephant Grass: The Nova Scotian term (especially connected to Annapolis County) for 'Phragmites australis,' a tall willowy grass, once used by the Acadians to thatch their roofs.

Eureka: Usually a term of exclamation. In Nova Scotia it is a small Pictou County town so-named for the Eureka Milling Company established there in 1883.

"Farewell to Nova Scotia": A folk song, and unofficial Nova Scotian Anthem.

"Fast as Snot": Really, really fast.

"Feed of Smelts": A springtime ritual, a feast of the fresh water fish, smelts.

Frenchys: A phenomenally successful chain of stores in Nova Scotia that sells used clothing from the Boston States.

"Going down the Road": Literally, going down the road, but this phrase mainly refers to people who are leaving the province to find work elsewhere, traditionally in Upper Canada, but more recently includes places like Alberta.

Giv'er: "Go for it."

Haligonian: Someone from the provincial capital, Halifax.

Hodge Podge: A Nova Scotian delicacy consisting of new garden vegetables boiled and bathed in cream.

Bio THOMAS CHANDLER HALIBURTON

Born in Windsor, Nova Scotia in 1796, Thomas Chandler Haliburton came from a long line of lawyers; both his father and grandfather practiced law. Like most young men in his privileged station, Haliburton attended university, graduating from King's College in Windsor in 1815.

In 1816, he married Louisa Neville, and together they had a total of 11 children, eight of them surviving infancy. By 1826, Haliburton had entered politics, becoming the representative for Annapolis Royal in the Nova Scotia Assembly, backing much of the Tory policy of the Upper House. His acerbic personality, quick wit, and sharp satire delighted his comrades in government as much as it enraged his political enemies. Many of the latter were relieved when he took a judgeship in 1829.

Changing Gears

This change in careers did not silence his keen political sensibility or clever ridicule of his opponents. Instead he now pursued his same targets in his writings. His history of Nova Scotia earned him much respect, but by far his most important work was his "Clockmaker" series, which appeared in Joseph Howe's Nova Scotian.

In 22 installments, these moral and satirical essays tell of the fictional Sam Slick of Slickville, a New England con-man who travelled through Nova Scotia, commenting (sometimes harshly) on what he saw. Slick is perhaps the most popular comic figure in nineteenth century English literature. In 1836, Howe collected these articles into a book called The Clockmaker, which proved to be wildly popular both in North America and in England. In 1854, ill health compelled Haliburton to retire, and he moved to England, where he was celebrated as an author and served as a member of parliament. He died in England in 1865.

"Haliburtanisms"
Sayings Coined by Nova Scotia's T.C. Haliburton

Thomas Chandler Haliburton was the toast of the British Empire. His success is said to have inspired another young writer with a similar wit by the name of Mark Twain. In introducing an international audience to a decidedly non-colonial take on life in North America, he created a new vocabulary rich is simile and metaphor that is still with us today. Here are just some examples.

- Raining cats and dogs
- Facts are stranger than fiction
- As quick as a wink
- Every dog has his day
- Drank like a fish
- Sharp as a needle
- You can't get blood from a stone
- Real skinflint
- Live and let live
- Give and take
- A stitch in time saves nine
- Barked up the wrong tree
- Flies off the handle
- Honesty is the best policy
- As large as life
- The early bird catches the worm
- I wasn't born yesterday
- An ounce of prevention is worth a pound of cure
- Jack of all trades and master of none
- Stick in the mud

HRM: The Halifax Regional Municipality, the amalgamated provincial capital (1996) consisting of the communities of Halifax, Dartmouth, Bedford and Sackville, as well as the county of Halifax.

Hurley: An early incarnation of hockey, played with a ball, not a puck, at Windsor, the birthplace of hockey.

Keith's: Properly, "Alexander Keith's Pale Ale," a popular beer made in Nova Scotia.

Kitchen Party: An informal gathering of friends and family which inevitably ends up in the kitchen, the focal point of Nova Scotian social life.

The L.C.: The Liquor Commission, where Nova Scotians buy their beer, such as Keiths, as well as wine and spirits.

Les Suetes: Southeasterly winds known to be especially fierce at Cheticamp, Cape Breton. Known to reach hurricane strength, these winds are often damaging, and warrant weather warnings. They are created when warm air moves over cool water. This front inversion creates a "funneling effect" over elevations like the Cape Breton Highlands and the air is forced to speed up, creating strong gusts as it comes down the side of the elevation.

MacPass: Electronic pass purchased, in lieu of using tokens or quarters, to facilitate crossing the Macdonald Bridge that connects Halifax and Dartmouth.

Me Son: Term of endearment, given by an elderly man in reference to a younger man (a literal kinship is not necessary).

Men of the Deeps: Generically, miners who toil in Cape Breton Coal mines, and also a world-renowned choir consisting of the same.

Mi-Carême: This Cape Breton mid-Lent celebration, adapted from ancient French custom, is designed to ease the drudgery of Lenten sacrifice. During Mi-Carême, people don costumes and visit their friends and families, who have to guess the identities of those in disguise.

Mug up: An evening cup o'tea.

NBA: In the perennial battle between CFAs (Come-From-Aways) and the local population, a CFA can respond — and often does — by calling the locals "NBAs" . . . Never-Been-Aways.

Nor'Easter: A strong coastal storm that requires cold air meeting warm, a source of moisture and a strong jet stream.

Oat Cakes: A hearty oat cookie, also called "Scotch Cakes."

Pizza Corner: A haven for pizza lovers in Halifax, this corner of the city at Blowers and Grafton Streets features three pizza joints at one intersection. The fourth corner offers a stone wall on which to sit and eat!

Poutine Râpée: Unlike the Quebec-originated concoction of french fries, cheese curd and gravy, this Acadian poutine is a baseball-sized ball of grated and mashed potato that is salted, stuffed with pork, boiled, then served with salt and pepper or brown sugar.

Rappie Pie: An Acadian comfort food, this is a dish of grated potatoes and stewed chicken.

Rear: A meaning of this word unique to Nova Scotia, especially Cape Breton, is its usage to denote the back section of a community, sections of land often deemed less desirable.

Rummies: Nova Scotians who, in the late nineteenth and early twentieth centuries, opposed the prohibition of alcohol.

Smashers: Nova Scotians who, in the late 19th and early 20th centuries, desired a prohibition on alcohol.

Sociable!: A social tradition in Nova Scotian bars. A sociable is the raising of glasses in unison, in response to the cry, "Sociable!"

Sou'Wester: A rain-slicker hat, worn by fishermen.

"Seattle East": Halifax, so-named because it, like Seattle, was home to a sizeable grunge music movement in the 1990s.

Skatist: Early Nova Scotian name for a skater.

Tarbish: A card game played primarily by the people in Cape Breton.

Timmy's/Tim's: Tim Hortons, a Canadian coffee shop chain, cofounded by Nova Scotian Ron Joyce from Tatamagouche, with a remarkably abundant Nova Scotia presence.

"The Valley": To Nova Scotians, the Annapolis Valley.

Tourtière: A traditional Acadian meat pie, served especially at Christmas.

Trailer Park Boys: A popular TV show set in a trailer park, with something of a cult following. The show, which traces the lives of a pathetic bunch of losers, is filmed in and around Halifax.

Triple-Triple: A coffee prepared with three creams, three sugars. In Nova Scotia this usually happens at Timmy's.

Two-four: A case of twenty-four beers.

Upper Canadian: Often pejorative, someone from Ontario.

White Juan: A term now indelibly ingrained in the Nova Scotia lexicon, this refers to the massive snow storm of February 18-19, 2004, which dropped up to 95 centimeters of snow on the province and brought fierce winds gusting to 120 km/hr. White Juan was reminiscent of the devastating Hurricane Juan, which tracked across the province the previous September.

Geography

Nova Scotia is the second smallest province in Canada, larger only than Prince Edward Island. Still, it is twice the size of Massachusetts and just a bit smaller than the country of Ireland. Its land mass accounts for 0.6 percent of Canada's total, but then again, Canada is the second largest country in the world behind Russia.

One of Nova Scotia's great historians, J. Murray Beck, describes the province as jutting out into the North Atlantic like some giant lobster-shaped pier. Indeed it is connected to mainland North America by a small isthmus only 24 kms across. One-fifth of the province's land mass consists of the island of Cape Breton Island.

SUM IS GREATER THAN THE PARTS

Nova Scotia wasn't Nova Scotia a billion years ago, of course. Nova Scotia was formed as a result of the coming together of a large mountainous land mass formed near the equator with another giant land mass with more desert-like qualities, formed 750 million years ago near the current South Pole. The result is that the province is divided in two by a diagonal fault-line that is a result of the coming together.

The real legacy manifests itself in three distinct terrains. First, there are the Atlantic uplands, which stretch all along the southern and eastern coastlines and as far as 80 kms inland. Their most striking feature is the rocky coastal shore, full of bays, coves and inlets. A second distinct terrain is the highlands, a series of mountainous regions lying alongside the Bay of Fundy and throughout much of Cape Breton Island. Finally, there are the lowlands of the Annapolis Valley and along the Northumberland Strait, often lying below sea level and forming the most fertile agricultural land in the province.

PHYSICAL SETTING
- Size: 55,490 km2
- Length: 575 km
- Average width: 128 km
- Furthest distance from the ocean: 56 km
- Length of shoreline: 7,579 km

NORTH POLE
Nova Scotia is located between 43° and 48° north latitude, and between 59° and 67° west longitude. This puts the province halfway between the equator and the North Pole. In fact, with a latitude of 45°08', the town of Stewiacke is almost precisely at the halfway point.

Take 5 TOP FIVE PEAKS
(ALL IN CAPE BRETON)

1. **White Hill** - 536m
2. **The Pinnacle** - 530m
3. **Grey Hill** - 464m
4. **John Peters Mountain** - 457m
5. **Icy Mountain** - 452m

SEEING THE TREES FOR THE FOREST

When the first European settlers came to Nova Scotia, the most prominent feature of the land was its dense mixed forests. Today, 77 percent of Nova Scotia's land mass is still woodland, amounting to 4.25 million hectares of forest. About one-fifth of this is Crown land.

- Percentage of forest lands that is Softwood: 54
- Hardwood: 13
- Mixed woods: 24
- Other: 9

Take 5   MICHAEL HAYNES'
FIVE FAVOURITE HIKES

Michael Haynes has made a name for himself doing what he loves best: hiking the hills, highlands and coastlines of Nova Scotia. He has supplied Nova Scotian hikers with such guides as *Hiking Trails of Nova Scotia*, *Hiking Trails of Cape Breton*, and *Trails of the Halifax Regional Municipality*. Born in Nova Scotia, Haynes currently lives in Ottawa where he administers a national trails website (www.TrailsCanada.com) for Go For Green, a foundation that promotes active living in the outdoors.

All Haynes' picks share some common elements: They are all challenging hikes, either in distance or in ruggedness; each is located in an isolated corner of the province, and so tends not to attract too many visitors; and all of them except Franey follow the coastline. If you're a fairly experienced hiker and you like wild, authentic Nova Scotia nature at its best, we suggest you give one of these hikes a try.

1. **Polletts Cove**, Inverness County
2. **Franey**, Cape Breton Highlands National Park
3. **Cape Chignecto Trail**, Cumberland County
4. **Taylor Head Provincial Park**, Halifax County
5. **Gabarus to Belfry Gut**, Cape Breton County

COMMERCIAL FORESTRY

- Percentage of Nova Scotian forest that is harvested commercially each year: 2
- Percentage of harvested areas that grow back naturally: 85
- Percentage that is reforested using seedlings: 15

MOTHER NATURE'S PRUNING

Every summer Nova Scotians can expect 400 to 500 forest fires. The most destructive forest fire season of recent times was 1976 when 17,536 hectares of forest burned.

FARM COUNTRY

With 77 percent of Nova Scotia covered in trees, three percent in wet-lands, and many coastal areas too rocky to grow anything, it leaves only ten percent of provincial lands suitable for agriculture. Three of the most productive areas are the lowlands of the Annapolis Valley, the shores of the Northumberland Strait, and the Margaree Valley in Cape Breton.

Acadian settlers were the first methodical farmers in the province. In the early 1600s they built intricate systems of dykes along the Fundy shore to claim rich, fertile soil from the sea. About 240 km of that dyke system still exists today, protecting 33,000 hectares of land, and over 600 residential and commercial buildings, from the Fundy tides.

WATER, WATER, EVERYWHERE

ISLANDS

- Number of coastal islands: 3,809
- Percentage of the provincial landmass that is made up of islands: 20
- Percentage of that accounted for by Cape Breton Island: 93

CAPE BRETON
- Length of Cape Breton Island: 175 km
- Width at its widest point: 135 km
- Rank of Cape Breton Island on the list of the largest islands in the world: 75
- Percentage of the Nova Scotia coastline accounted for by Cape Breton Island: 25

BEACHES
The warmest beaches in Nova Scotia are along the shores of the Northumberland Strait. The waters in the Strait are shallow enough that they heat up faster in the summer than beaches along the Atlantic coast.

- Number of publicly accessible beaches in the province: over 100
- Number of people who visit Nova Scotia's public beaches each year: 250,000-500,000

WATER
- Percentage of the total landmass of Nova Scotia that is fresh water: 3.5
- Number of lakes larger than one hectare: 6,600
- Number of lakes greater than 1000 square meters: 38,242 Lakes + 67 River Lakes
- Number of major rivers: 166

Did you know...

That in 1985 the largest fossil find ever in North America was unearthed on the north shore of the Minas Basin, near Parrsboro? More than 100,000 fossil specimens — some more than 200 million years old — were found, including a series of dinosaur footprints, each the size of a penny.

TOP FIVE PEAKS
IN MAINLAND NOVA SCOTIA

1. **Nuttby Mountain** - 361m
2. **Higgins Mountain** - 360m
3. **Dalhousie Mountain** - 341m
4. **Stevens Mountain** - 339m
5. **Sugarloaf Mountain** - 319m

LARGEST . . .

• LAKE in the province is Bras d'Or Lake in Cape Breton, which covers about one-tenth of the Island. But being in such close proximity to the ocean, it actually holds salt water, making it the largest saltwater lake in North America.

• HARBOUR in the province is Halifax Harbour, which is about 8 km long. At its mouth it's about 2 km wide, with a narrow channel that leads to a huge inner harbour. This also makes Halifax harbour the second largest in the world after Sydney, Australia, and, at a depth of 18 meters at low tide, one of the deepest harbours in the world, and the harbour with the largest water volume in the world.

OFFSHORE
The sea, or offshore, is a defining characteristic of Nova Scotia. With the adoption of the 200-mile limit in 1977, the offshore segment of the

Did you know...

That there are more than 300 species of seaweed around Nova Scotia coasts? Seaweed growth occurs most abundantly on the rocky shores of the Atlantic coast. The main seaweeds attaching to rocks are the kelps and rockweeds. Eelgrass prefers the soft bottoms of protected inlets and bays, especially in the Northumberland Strait.

Take 5 TOP FIVE LONGEST RIVERS
IN NOVA SCOTIA

1. **West River St. Marys** - 118 km
2. **Mersey River** - 115 km
3. **Tusket River** - 112 km
4. **Annapolis River** - 102 km
5. **Medway River**- 100 km

province — an area of almost 400,000 square kms — is larger than the land portion by a magnitude of four. The straits, seas and, of course, the Atlantic Ocean are more than just geological descriptors, they are an important influence on how Nova Scotians see themselves and how many people outside the province view them.

CONTINENTAL SHELF AND SLOPE

Beyond Nova Scotia's coastline lies an underwater continental shelf that extends like a submerged coastal plain from 125 to 230 km seaward. The average depth is 90 meters, with deeper basins and troughs that descend more than 200 meters.

Bordering the shelf are the deeper ocean waters of the continental slope that quickly descend to depths of over three kilometers. The major offshore areas making up the continental shelf are the Northumberland Strait, southeastern Gulf of St. Lawrence, Sydney Bight, Scotian Shelf, Georges Bank, Gulf of Maine, and the Bay of Fundy. A major feature of the shelf is a series of shallow banks that culminate at Sable Island, a 41 kilometer-long spit of land rising just 26 meters above sea level.

Did you know...

That Georges Bank, the large elevated section of the continental shelf off the coast of Nova Scotia and Maine, was actually a part of the North American mainland during the glacial period known as the Wisconsin Glaciation.

BANKING ON IT

The most productive of Nova Scotia's offshore banks is Georges Bank, located midway between Cape Sable and Cape Cod. Here the relative shallowness of the water, coupled with the warming effect of the Gulf Stream, creates a flourishing environment for marine animal and plant

Take 5 SILVER DONALD'S
FIVE FAVOURITE CAPE BRETON BEACHES

Silver Donald Cameron is one of Nova Scotia's most gifted writers. His books have ranged over subjects as diverse as the fishery and economic development to his award-winning *The Living Beach*. Cameron is an inveterate traveller and has stepped foot on some of the world's best beaches. Here he gives us the low-down on the best beaches on one of the most beautiful islands in the world. Cameron's books are available at Breton Books. Like any shrewd fisherman, though, Cameron ain't telling anyone his favourite beach.

1. **Port Hood**. A classic sandy swimming beach, reached through a municipal park, Port Hood Beach is easily accessible from the Ceilidh Trail, and fronts on the warm salt water of the Gulf of St. Lawrence. Directly across from the beach is Port Hood Island, whose old houses have been preserved as summer homes – and which has beaches equally appealing. Similar beaches extend all along the Gulf shore from the New Brunswick border to Cheticamp.

2. **Point Michaud**. A cold, fog-draped Atlantic beach, Point Michaud is a long arc of fine grey sand backed by low grassy dunes, with only a sprinkling of homes and cottages. Point Michaud itself is a tombolo, an eroding headland connected to the Cape Breton shore by a neck of sand, with beaches on both sides. Gannets fish offshore, and easterly gales create a magnificent surf. The water is often bitingly cold. The main beach is perhaps a mile and a half in length, but even on a hot Canada Day fewer than 100 people were frisking on it. It's often completely deserted.

life. It is the most westward of the great Atlantic fishing banks that stretch all the way to the Grand Banks of Newfoundland.

At one time Georges Bank was home to the largest herring stocks in the world. Today it supports several Nova Scotian fisheries, including scallop, lobster, groundfish, swordfish and tuna.

3. **Cape George**. Cape George, on the Bras d'Or Lakes, is not to be confused with the other Cape George near Antigonish. (Why did our ancestors do this?) A double tombolo, Cape George is linked to the adjoining land by two beaches with a barachois lagoon trapped between them. The twin gravel beaches separate the warm salty water of the Lakes from the warm fresh water of the barachois. Cruising in Silversark, I like to go ashore with a bar of soap, and use the lagoon as a vast bathtub.

4. **Marble Mountain**. Also on the Bras d'Or Lakes, Marble Mountain is unique: a beach of white marble fragments which drops steeply into crystal-clear water at the base of high cliffs where limestone once was quarried. Cruising yachts from all over the world stop here, and the offshore waters are crowded with wooded islands which can easily be reached with a kayak or an inflatable. North America's most easterly and northerly vineyard is nearby – not, alas, open to the public, but a testimony to the relative mildness of the summer climate.

5. **Pondville Beach**. On the eastern shore of Isle Madame, Pondville Beach is my home beach, a complete beach system stretching seven miles between the tree-line and the deep water. A little stream nourishes it with sediments from the middle of the island, and the tiny reed-rimmed estuary makes a children's swimming hole. A small lagoon behind the low dunes sustains muskrats and water birds. Most of the beach is sandy, but in one spot big cobbles roll in the surf, clacking and rattling in the backwash.

Weather

WEATHER

Predicting the weather in Nova Scotia is not for the faint of heart. Mark Twain could very easily have been talking about Nova Scotia when he said if you don't like the weather, just wait a minute. Winds moving eastward from the interior of the continent combined with the mixing of two major ocean currents — the Labrador Current, bringing the cold waters of the North Atlantic, and the Gulf Stream, bringing warm waters from the Gulf of Mexico — make it a witch's brew that confounds even the best of meteorologists.

What this all means is that as a result of cool waters springtime weather is marked by similarly cool winds, often extending the spring season into June. The upside is that late springs develop into late autumns, with the now-warmer waters giving Nova Scotians an extra boost before Old Man Winter sets in.

TEMPERATURES
- Spring: 2° to 9° C
- Summer: 16° to 24° C
- Autumn: 12° to 18° C
- Winter: -3° to -6° C
- Coldest month of the year: February
- Warmest month of the year: July

Did you know...

- That the area of Browns Bank, 60 km south of Cape Sable, is visited by about 200 Northern Right Whales each year.

- That the Georges Bank scallop stock is the largest in the world.

AND THE WINNER IS . . .

- Record high: August 19, 1935 in Collegeville, Guysborough County: 38.3° C

- Record low: January 31, 1921 in Upper Stewiacke: -41.1° C

SUNSHINE

- Average number of days of sun per year: 160

RAIN

- Average number of rainy days per year: 170
- Average annual rainfall amount: 1,178 millimeters

GROWING SEASON

- Growing season: May to September
- Number of frost-free days per year in Nova Scotia: 120
- In the farmlands of the Annapolis Valley: 140
- Highlands of Cape Breton Island: 100

SNOW

- Percentage of annual precipitation that falls as snow: 15
- Average number of days per year there is snow on the ground somewhere in Nova Scotia: 110
- Average amount of snow that falls each year along the coast: 150 cm
- Inland: 250 cm
- In northern Cape Breton: 300 cm

Bay of Fundy

The way author Esther Shephard tells it in her version of the old legend, it was the mythical giant Paul Bunyan who first caused the great tides to run in the Bay of Fundy — the infant Paul Bunyan at that!

"Paul was asleep in his cradle when they went to get him," she wrote, "and they had to send for the British navy and it took seven hours of bombardin' to wake him up. And when Paul stepped out of his cradle it made such a swell it caused a 75-foot tide in the Bay of Fundy and several villages was swept away and seven of the invincible English warships was sunk to the bottom of the sea."

The great cataclysm passed and Paul moved on, but, Shephard wrote, "the tides in the Bay of Fundy is just as high as they ever was."

Indeed, the tides of the Bay of Fundy are the largest in the world, rising some 16 meters, or the equivalent of a four-storey building. Twice a day, 200 billion tonnes of water enter and leave the Bay of Fundy, an amount equal to all the rivers on Earth.

The tidal exchange of the Bay of Fundy means the waters stretching as far as Georges Bank get a twice-daily vertical mixing, making the waters nutritionally rich and the fishing grounds enormously productive. (Unfortunately for some parts of southwestern Nova Scotia, it also makes it the fog capital of the province.)

The Bay of Fundy is in part responsible for sustaining a large herring stock off southwestern Nova Scotia. Lobster and scallop fisheries also benefit from the Fundy tides and these fisheries are the most important industry in many of the communities that dot the shoreline.

Did you know...

PASS THE SHOVEL

- Heaviest one-day snowfall was on February 19, 2004 in Halifax when 95 cm fell. Following as it did on the heels of Hurricane Juan, Nova Scotians dubbed it White Juan.
- Largest snowfall amount in one season was in the winter of 1964-5 when a total of 653 cm of the white stuff fell in Cheticamp.

WINDS

- Spring and summer winds typically blow from south or southwest at speeds of 10 to 15 km/h.
- Autumn and winter winds typically blow from west and northwest at speeds of 20 to 25 km/h.

LES SUETES

Along the western shores of Cape Breton, especially around Cheticamp and Grand Etang, there's a local wind phenomenon known as les suetes. These sudden windstorms are well known in the area for the wide destruction they can cause. They occur when warm air off the ocean collides with the cold air of the Cape Breton Highlands. The air swirls together and descends eastward down the mountains, gathering speed as it goes. The strongest suete ever recorded happened on March 13, 1993, blowing at 233 km/hour.

Did you know...

Nova Scotia's Most Famous Sandbar

Although most Nova Scotians have never been to Sable Island, it holds a mythical place in their hearts and minds. And little wonder why. It sits in the Atlantic Ocean some 300 kilometers southeast of Halifax, orphaned and with no permanent residents, yet by some historical quirk of fate, 250 horses roam the island freely, persevering and even reveling in its punishing climate.

The crescent shaped island is only 38 kilometers long and 1.5 kilometers wide at its widest. Three major ocean currents – the Labrador, the Belle Isle and the Gulf Stream – converge around it, mixing a brew of warm and cold waters that means it is covered in fog for more than a third of the year.

Adding to Sable's mystique are the more than 350 shipwrecks that have happened off its shores. Sailors, privateers, convicts and pirates have all been temporary residents here. In one incident, forty convicts were shipwrecked here in 1598, and when their rescuers came some five years later that number had shrunk to 12. There has been no accounting of the lives taken by Sable, but in two consecutive years, 1926 and 1927, the Lunenburg fishing fleet alone lost 138 men.

There were many stories told back on land of deliberate wrecks, where "wreckers" crashed their vessels, murdering their passengers only to make away with their valuables. It was these "wreckers" that prompted the government to build the first lighthouse in 1873 (it had to be moved five times because of erosion), and it remained staffed until the 1960s.

Islands have always captured writers' imaginations and Sable is no different. Nova Scotia's most celebrated writer, Thomas Raddall, had worked on Sable Island as a young man, and much of the plot for his book The Nymph and the Lamp was set on Sable. Other writers, like Barbara Christie and Marq deVilliers, have followed in Raddall's footsteps.

HARNESSING THE WIND

Nova Scotia's first wind powered electrical generating facility opened in May 2005 at Pubnico Point. The state-of-the-art wind farm is expected to generate about 100 million kW/h of electricity per year. That's enough to power about 13,000 households, reducing carbon dioxide emissions from Nova Scotia's coal power plants by about 90,000 tonnes per year. Another 19-turbine wind project on the Tantramar Marshes is scheduled to be up and running by 2007.

Take 5 PETER COADE'S
FIVE THINGS YOU DIDN'T KNOW ABOUT NOVA SCOTIA WEATHER

Peter Coade has been studying weather since joining the federal government's weather service in 1962. He has worked at centers in Nova Scotia, Newfoundland (Goose Bay) and Ontario. Immediately prior to 'returning home' to Halifax and becoming a familiar face to viewers of ATV/ASN in Atlantic Canada, Coade was the manager of the Toronto Weather Office. While in Toronto, he was also the staff meteorologist for CFRB radio station, working alongside such personalities as the late Gordon Sinclair and Betty Kennedy (of Front Page Challenge fame) and was the Air Committee meteorologist for the Canadian International Air Show (CIAS/CNE).

1. Wind is a significant factor on the plateau of the Cape Breton Highlands, and also on the west coast (Inverness County) where winds from the southeast – locally called les suetes – typically reach hurricane force, gusting up to 200 kilometers per hour. High southeast winds gain speed over the open plateau and tumble down onto the western coast in turbulent gusts, buffeting local communities.

FOG

The number of potentially sunny days in the province each year is decreased by fifty percent because of fog.

- Longest stretch of fog ever recorded was 85 days in the summer of 1967 in the town of Yarmouth.
- Number of days Yarmouth was without fog that summer: 7

2. The highest tides on Earth occur in the Minas Basin, the eastern extremity of the Bay of Fundy, where the average tide range is 12 meters and can reach 17 meters when the various factors affecting the tides are in phase.

3. Nova Scotia is almost an island, with no point in the province more than 60 km from the water. In the late spring and early summer, warm southerly breezes produce extensive fog along the Atlantic coast, but that short drive to the other side of the province reveals warmth and sunshine. It is the effect of these same southerly breezes blowing in off the cold North Atlantic that inhibit the production of severe thunderstorms and tornadoes – a rarity in the province.

4. Although Nova Scotia has what is termed a "maritime climate", it is greatly modified in certain months of the year to possess a "continental climate. As a result, temperature extremes on record vary from near –40°C in the depths of winter to near +40°C in the summer months.

5. According to the publication, *The Climate of Canada*, Nova Scotia is called "the Stormiest Province.

1. **Sable Island:** 152 days
2. **Halifax:** 122 days per year
3. **Yarmouth:** 118 days
4. **Canso:** 115 days
5. **Dartmouth:** 101 days

STORMS

The earliest storm ever recorded in Nova Scotia was the Great Hurricane of August 1635 that hit the coast of Massachusetts on its northward track, wrecking ships arriving with new colonists and destroying thousands of huge trees. It then passed through Nova Scotia near Cape Sable.

CAN YOU SAY CYCLONE?

A disastrous tropical cyclone that struck Cape Breton Island in 1873 led to the establishment of a Canadian storm warning system. Residents were caught so unprepared for the storm that over 500 lives were lost, 1,200 vessels sank, and 900 buildings were damaged or leveled. At the time, losses were estimated at $3.5 million, equivalent to about $70 million today. The telegraph service at the time had momentarily been interrupted, preventing storm warnings from Toronto getting to Halifax, helping to convince officials of the need to establish a separate storm warning system for Canada.

Did you know...

That there are over 150 lighthouses in Nova Scotia, which give ships at sea a beacon of light through the fog and the dark of the night? At one time they were staffed by lighthouse keepers, but today they are all automated.

CAN YOU SAY NOR'EASTER?
- Typical Nor'easter wind speed: 150 km/h
- Typical peak wave heights: 14 m
- Amount of snow a Nor'easter typically brings: 25 cm

HURRICANES AND TROPICAL STORMS
- Average number that affect Atlantic Canada each year: 3 or 4
- Last year in which a Category 4 or 5 hurricane struck Nova Scotia: 1851
- Number of Category 2 hurricanes that have struck Nova Scotia in the past 110 years: 2

Tornadoes are extremely rare in Nova Scotia. The last major one reported was in Liverpool on January 30, 1954, which was accompanied by heavy hail and lightning.

BRING IT JUAN
The most destructive storm in Nova Scotia's history occurred on September 29, 2003, a Category 2 hurricane named Juan. Having quietly crept up the eastern seaboard from its birthplace in Bermuda, this storm landed at about midnight, walloping Nova Scotia and carving a path of destruction through Halifax and Truro.

With maximum sustained winds of 151 km/h, and maximum winds gusts of 176 km/h gusts, literally millions of trees in the province were uprooted. That included over 70 percent - 55,000 - of the trees in Halifax's scenic Point Pleasant Park. The seas surged about two meters

Did you know...

That the most winter lightning in Canada occurs in an area just south of Sable Island in the Atlantic Ocean? Here, the cold air from the Arctic collides with the warm air of the Gulf of Mexico, creating ideal conditions for thunderstorms and lightning.

Did you know...

along the coastline, while the maximum wave height recorded during the storm reached almost 20 m.

Between 800,000 to 900,000 residents of Nova Scotia and Prince Edward Island lost power at some point during the storm, and it took Nova Scotia Power over two weeks to restore power to all its customers. In total, Juan caused over $200 million worth of damage to the province in a period of just three hours. Eight people were killed as a result of the storm.

WHITE JUAN

With the memories of Hurricane Juan still fresh in folks' minds, the fiercest winter storm ever to strike Nova Scotia occurred the following winter, on February 18th and 19th, 2004. Snowfall records were shattered. Winds reaching near record levels shut down the province for days afterward.

- Amount of snow that fell across Nova Scotia: 60 to 90 cm
- Amount that typically accumulated per hour during the storm: 7 cm
- Amount that typically accumulates per hour during a normal winter storm in Nova Scotia: 2 to 3 cm
- Maximum wind gusts recorded during the storm: 124 km/hr
- Amount of snow that fell in:
- Halifax and Dartmouth: 95.5 cm
- Sydney: 40.8 cm
- Yarmouth: 82.6 cm

Did you know...

Take 5 TOP FIVE MOST DESTRUCTIVE HURRICANES IN NOVA SCOTIA

1. **Hurricane Juan** - 2003
2. **Hurricane Edna** - 1954
3. **Hurricane Carol** - 1953
4. **Great Atlantic Hurricane** - 1944
5. **Portland Gale** - 1898

EARTHQUAKES

Earthquakes in Nova Scotia are rare, and mostly occur off the coast. Since 1954, 21 minor earthquakes have been recorded on the ocean floor, registering between 1.7 and 3.8 on the Richter scale.

The only earthquake to result in any major damage in Nova Scotia occurred off the coast of Newfoundland in 1929, which generated a tidal wave that struck Cape Breton Island. Though spared the widespread coastal devastation suffered by Newfoundland, one Cape Bretoner was killed and minor damage was done to the shoreline and seaside homes.

Perhaps the most famous earthquake to have ever been felt in Nova Scotia was the great Lisbon earthquake of 1755, off the coast of Portugal, which caused a few minor tremors along the Nova Scotia shoreline

Did you know...

That strange weather isn't the only weird thing that happens in the sky over Nova Scotia? According to the researchers at the University of Manitoba, there were 23 reported sightings of UFOs in the skies over Nova Scotia during 2004.

Politics

With the Treaty of Paris in 1763, France essentially ceded political domain to England for all of North America. Initially, Cape Breton Island, Prince Edward Island, and New Brunswick were joined to Nova Scotia, but later (1769) P.E.I. was separated from Nova Scotia, as were Cape Breton Island and New Brunswick in 1784. Cape Breton Island would be re-annexed in 1820.

Nova Scotia achieved present day Canada's first representative assembly, with elections taking place for the first time in 1758 in Halifax. Nova Scotia was far from democratic, but it at least now had a bicameral legislature that included an elected house of assembly. Although the elected assembly clamoured for more and more authority, it was the council appointed by the Crown that had final legislative, judicial, and executive powers.

REFORMERS

By 1820, reformers were demanding responsible government, meaning they wanted real autonomy for the legislative branch. The leader who would make it happen was the influential orator and publisher, Joseph Howe, who used his newspaper and his powerful speaking skills to challenge the governor. In 1848, the governor finally relented and Nova Scotia became the first British colony to obtain responsible government.

CANADA CALLING

Great Britain was looking for a way to maintain some influence in North America and at the same time create a counterpoint to the increasingly powerful American democracy. The solution was to consolidate their North American sphere of influence in the British North America Act, in effect creating the country of Canada.

Support for confederation in Nova Scotia was tepid. Nova Scotia's elite saw their fortunes more closely entwined with that of Great Britain than with a newly imagined country. When the first election was called, 18 of the 19 Nova Scotians elected to the new federal House of Commons opposed Confederation.

The chief opposition spokesman was none other than Joseph Howe. In the end, however, the forces aligned against Howe and his colleagues were just too huge to overcome.

POST CONFEDERATION

In 1928, Nova Scotia abolished its appointed council, in effect vesting all legislative authority in the elected assembly. The province operates in the British parliamentary tradition with the government staying in power as long as it has the support of the majority of the members of the legislature. There are no fixed dates for elections, but tradition dictates that a government cannot go without calling an election within five years of the beginning of its mandate.

They Said It

> "The few members who watched the British North America Act in its speedy passage through parliament could scarcely conceal their excruciating boredom, and after the ordeal was over, they turned with lively zeal and manifest relief to the great national problem of the tax on dogs."
>
> **– Historian Donald Creighton's take on the 'momentous' signing of the BNA Act, in The Victorians and the Empire, 1937**

Take 5 DR. J. MURRAY BECK'S
FIVE MOST IMPORTANT POLITICAL
FIGURES IN NOVA SCOTIA HISTORY

Born in Lunenburg in 1914, Dr. J. Murray Beck has taught and written extensively on Canadian and Nova Scotian government and
political history. He is Professor Emeritus of Political Science at
Dalhousie University. Among his books are *Joseph Howe, Vol. I
and Vol. II*, The Government of Nova Scotia, and the two-volume
Politics of Nova Scotia.

1. **Joseph Howe**. Led a non-violent reform movement in Nova
Scotia during the 1830s and 1840s. As a result, in February 1848,
the province became the first colony in the British Empire to achieve
responsible government.

2. **Robert L. Stanfield**. As Premier of Nova Scotia from 1956 to 1967,
Robert Stanfield's successful promotion of industrial development led
to his recognition as a prime mover in building the 'new Nova Scotia.'
As opposition leader at Ottawa between 1967 and 1976, he won the
reputation of being "the best prime minister Canada never had."

3. **Angus L. Macdonald**. Premier of Nova Scotia from 1933 to 1940
and from 1945 to 1954, had a natural eloquence and gifts of intellect
and judgment leading to "a wide personal following not seen in the
province since the days of Howe." Perhaps his hold over Nova
Scotians was even stronger than that of Howe.

4. **George H. Murray**. Even in the absence of polls, had an uncanny
aptitude for gauging the attitudes and sensibilities of the Nova Scotia
people. That enabled him to win six successive elections and hold the
premiership for twenty-six years from 1896 to 1923, a time still
unequalled in the annals of British parliamentary government.

5. **Sir Robert Borden**. Headed the government of Canada during
the First World War. Under him, the country took tentative steps
leading in the next decade to full Canadian autonomy.

HE SAID/HE SAID

"He appeared deeply impressed by my statements, and said great many civil things, but expressed his fears that if he took that course his party would abandon him."

—Charles Tupper, in an April 9, 1868 letter to John A. Macdonald, describing an earlier meeting with Joseph Howe in which he had tried to convince Howe to abandon his anti-Confederation stance.

"He thinks the Canadians will offer us any terms, and that he and I combined might rule the Dominion. Of course I gave him no satisfaction."

—Joseph Howe's decidedly less enthusiastic interpretation of this same meeting with Tupper, in a letter to Macdonald dated April 9, 1868.

PARTIES

Two main political parties in Nova Scotia, the Liberal Party and the Progressive Conservative Party, have governed the province since its entry into Canada. The Liberals have been in power the lion's share of the time. During the 20th century, the Liberals governed until 1925, from 1933 to 1956, 1970 to 1978, and 1993 to 1999; the Progressive Conservatives were in power during the other periods. The Progressive Conservatives regained control of the provincial government in 1999. In the late 1990s, the New Democratic Party (NDP) increased its share of seats in the House of Assembly.

PREMIER PRIMER

Nova Scotia has had a total of 29 premiers in its history. Sixteen have been Liberals and 13 Conservatives. In case you are a counter, 19 premiers were lawyers, five were newspaper editors and five were farmers, but only one had a Black Belt-Fourth dan degree in TaeKwon Do (Russell MacLellan).

Take 5 PREMIER RODNEY MACDONALD'S
FIVE FAVOURITE NOVA SCOTIANS

Rodney MacDonald was born January 2, 1972 in Inverness, Nova Scotia. Upon graduating from high school in Mabou, Inverness County, MacDonald earned a Bachelor of Science in Physical Education from St. Francis Xavier University.

MacDonald was elected to Nova Scotia Legislature July 1999 as the MLA for Inverness. In February 2006, MacDonald won the leadership race for the Nova Scotia Progressive Conservative party and was sworn in as the province,s 26th Premier. Nova Scotians re-elected MacDonald Premier in 2006.

MacDonald previously worked as a teacher and a professional musician -- receiving two nominations for East Coast Music Awards.

1. **John Hamm** - His courage and conviction to balance the budget for the first time in 40 years has given our province a better, more prosperous future.

2. **Alex Angus MacDonald** - My father influenced me greatly over the course of my life. A municipal coucillor and pipefitter, his advice and example provided me with direction both personally and professionally.

3. **Maud Lewis** - Her physical challenges due to arthritis and polio did not discourage her efforts to express her artistic talents. Her paintings indicate a positive spirit revealing the simple everyday beauty of life.

4. **Angus L. MacDonald** - Young, impressive, well educated and highly charismatic, his leadership brought stability to Nova Scotia through the Depression era. One of his greatest achievements was the establishment of a public education system for all Nova Scotians.

5. **Al MacInnis** - Al has had a spectacular career and will be regarded as one of the NHL's finest defensemen of all time. He had talent, but he also dedicated himself to the discipline of hard work. He went on to win the Stanley Cup and Conn Smythe Trophy as playoff MVP, as well as the Norris Trophy as the NHL's best defenseman.

Bio ANGUS L. MACDONALD

Born to a farming family in Dunvegan, Cape Breton in August 1890, Angus Lewis Macdonald was the ninth of fourteen children. Always studious, as a teenager Macdonald worked a range of jobs, saving every penny to pay his tuition at St. Francis Xavier University.

With the outbreak of World War I, Macdonald quickly enlisted. Just four days before Armistice, he was shot and critically wounded. When he regained his health, he returned to Nova Scotia, enrolling at Dalhousie Law School. He excelled at law school and, not long after graduating, became a popular law professor.

In 1930, Macdonald reluctantly accepted the leadership of the Nova Scotia Liberals. By 1933, he and his party handily won the provincial election with a mandate promising an Old Age Pension Act, support for workers' rights to unionize, and a plan to reduce government expenditures.

War Calling

During the Second World War, Macdonald handed off his premiership to Alexander MacMillan while he served in Ottawa as federal Minister of National Defence and Naval Services. In 1945, Macdonald returned to Nova Scotia politics, and, with the campaign slogan "All's well with Angus L" was again elected premier, this time with the largest mandate in Nova Scotia history.

Macdonald responded to calls for improved education for Nova Scotians by creating the province's first Department of Education. He embarked on major construction projects, including the first bridge connecting Halifax and Dartmouth, and the Canso Causeway. In the 1953 election, Macdonald was again elected. On April 11, 1954, 63-year old Macdonald had a heart attack, dying in his sleep two days later. Shocked Nova Scotians publicly mourned his death. In a state funeral held in Halifax, tens of thousands came to pay their final respects.

PREMIERS

NAME	PARTY	PROFESSION	SERVED
Hiram Blanchard	(confederate) Conservative	lawyer	July to Sept. 1867
William Annand	(anti-confederate) Liberal	farmer, newspaper editor	1867-75
Philip Hill	Liberal	lawyer, former Halifax mayor	1875-78
Simon Holmes	Conservative	lawyer, newspaper editor	1878-82
Sir John Thompson	Conservative	lawyer	May to July 1882
William Pipes	Liberal	lawyer	1882-84
William Fielding	Liberal	newspaper editor	1884-96
George H. Murray	Liberal	lawyer	1896-1923
Ernest Armstrong	Liberal	lawyer	1923-25
Edgar Rhodes	Conservative	lawyer	1925-30
Gordon Harrington	Conservative	lawyer	1930-35

Did you know...

That it wasn't until 1961 that Nova Scotia elected its first woman, Gladys Porter, to the Nova Scotia Legislature.

NAME	PARTY	PROFESSION	SERVED
Angus L. MacDonald	Liberal	barrister, lecturer, professor	1933-40; 1945-54
Alexander MacMillan	Liberal	businessman	1940-45
Harold Connolly	Liberal	newspaper editor	April to Sept. 1954
Henry Hicks	Liberal	lawyer	1954-56
Robert Stanfield	Conservative	lawyer	1956-67
George I. Smith	Conservative	lawyer	1967-70
Gerald Regan	Liberal	lawyer	1970-78
John Buchanan	Conservative	lawyer	1978-90
Roger Bacon	Conservative	farmer	1990-91
Donald Cameron	Conservative	farmer	1991-93
John Savage	Liberal	medical doctor	1993-97
Russell MacLellan	Liberal	lawyer	1997-99
John Hamm	Conservative	medical doctor	1999-

Did you know...

That three of Canada's first eight Prime Ministers were from Nova Scotia? They were John Sparrow David Thompson, Charles Tupper and Robert Laird Borden.

Did you know...

• That Premier Robert Stanfield was married to one of the grand-daughters of Premier Simon Holmes.

• That Prime Minister John Thompson died on his 50th birthday, November 10, 1894, from a sudden stroke during lunch at Windsor Castle, after being knighted that morning by Queen Victoria. His death challenged royal protocol. After holding a requiem mass for him at the castle, the Queen insisted his body be transported back to Canada with due pomp and ceremony. The HMS Blenheim was painted black for the journey across the Atlantic to Halifax, where a state funeral took place on January 3, 1895.

• That Premier John Thompson was the first Catholic Conservative Premier of Nova Scotia and the first Catholic Prime Minister of Canada. His religion prevented him from directly succeeding Sir John A. MacDonald.

• That George H. Murray was the longest serving premier in Nova Scotian and Canadian history, serving for 27 consecutive years from 1896 until finally resigning in 1923.

• That before Robert Stanfield was born, his family made a fortune selling the first unshrinkable underwear to Maritimers heading northwest to the Klondike Gold Rush. As a result, the young Robert never had to work, inheriting $350,000 at the age of 25 after his father died when he was 17.

• That Premier Robert Stanfield is one of only five Canadians carrying the Right Honourable title who wasn't a prime minister.

• That Nova Scotia had two premiers, Charles Tupper and Sir John Thompson, who went on to become Prime Ministers.

Then and Now

THE NAME FOR NOVA SCOTIA

From time immemorial, the Mi'kmaq knew their territory, including Nova Scotia, as Mi'kma'ki. From the time of French settlement in 1605, the French knew the region as l'Acadie. After the 1713 Treaty of Utrecht gave Nova Scotia to Britain, the region became known as Nova Scotia.

POPULATION

Before Europeans came to North America, Nova Scotia may have been home to as many as 75,000 Mi'kmaq or more. In 1605, Nova Scotia was home to about 44 Europeans and perhaps 3,000 Mi'kmaq, whose numbers had been dramatically reduced by European disease.

In 1901, there were 8.56 Nova Scotians per square kilometer, in 1951, 11.96 and today, 16.95 people per square kilometer.

WAGES

Average weekly salary of Nova Scotians in 1939: $21.42
- In 1959: $60.17
- Today: $597.00

NOVA SCOTIA WOMEN

The first recorded European woman to come to Nova Scotia arrived aboard a French vessel that landed in Acadia in 1636. This poor woman was vastly outnumbered by her male countrymen. Over the course of 369 years, the tables have turned. Today Nova Scotian women outnumber men – for every 100 women in the province there are 93.6 men.

Women are increasingly playing roles in Nova Scotia public life, too. In 1918, most Nova Scotian women got the right to vote and, although it took a while, in 1960 Gladys M. Porter became the first woman elected to the Nova Scotia legislature. In 1981, New Democrat Alexa McDonough became the first woman to head a provincial party. By 1991, more than half of the province's elected mayors were women. Although women represent 52 percent of the population, they comprise just 13.5 percent of Nova Scotia MLAs.

FARMING

Farming was once practiced by most Nova Scotians, either as a primary livelihood or part-time as a means of supplementing incomes and feeding families. Over the past century, the once-numerous Nova Scotia family farm has given way to fewer but larger, more efficient and mechanized farms.

- 1901 combined hectares of all Nova Scotia farms: 2,460,903
- In 1951: 1,284,477
- In 2001: 407,047

The output of efficient mammoth farms remains economically significant, but far fewer Nova Scotians live a farming lifestyle. In 1901, 52,836 Nova Scotians worked in agriculture. This number fell to 22,918 in 1951 and is approximately 9,000 today.

HOW 'BOUT THEM APPLES

Today, Nova Scotia apples are an important cash crop for the province. What many people don't know is that apples are not native to the province – they were introduced by Europeans in 1606. It was not until 1849 that Nova Scotia exported its first apples. Today, Nova Scotia

Halifax Explosion

December 6th, 1917 dawned a typical day in wartime Halifax as the harbour bustled with navy vessels, cargo ships and ferries. That morning, the Mont Blanc sailed into Halifax harbour, its cargo of explosives unmarked. As it approached its mooring, the Imo, a Belgian relief vessel, started down the harbour, crossing paths with the munitions ship.

Claiming the right-of-way, the Mont Blanc directed the Imo to move aside; the Imo stayed its course. In a final effort to avoid collision, the Mont Blanc veered left and the Imo threw its engines into reverse. It was too late and at 8:45 a.m. the two ships collided, igniting a fire aboard the Mont Blanc. Unaware of the deadly cargo, land and sea crews worked to quell flames, but at 9:04 a.m., as Haligonians watched on, the Mont Blanc exploded.

The largest manmade blast in history rained red-hot iron and steel down on the city. Moments later, a tsunami swept ashore. Homes, schools and businesses within two square kilometers of the Halifax waterfront were immediately obliterated and others destroyed by gas-line fires burning across the city. Firefighters and physicians from across Nova Scotia, Canada, and New England descended to offer immediate help, while relief committees were established to aid survivors, 6,000 of whom were left homeless.

The toll of the blast was staggering. Fifteen hundred people were killed instantly, hundreds more died in the aftermath, and an additional 9,000 were injured. In all, 1,630 buildings were destroyed and 12,000 damaged. It is estimated that in today's money, the Halifax explosion would have cost $430 million.

produces 100 million pounds of apples and each May Nova Scotians celebrate the fruit with the Apple Blossom Festival.

EDUCATION

In 1780, the first Nova Scotia law mandated the creation of publicly funded schools for poor children; everyone else had to pay for their children's schooling. Universal free public education arrived in 1864. Up until the 1950s, most Nova Scotians were educated in one-room school houses. With the advent of school busses in the 1950s, however, one-room schools were replaced with larger consolidated institutions.

- Number of children enrolled in Nova Scotia public schools in 1900: 98,000
- In 1950: 135,000
- In 2002/03: 150,599

FISHING

The fishery, like farming, has declined as a Nova Scotia employer. This is largely due to reductions in fish stocks, especially cod, a consequence of over-fishing. It is estimated that since the 1850s heyday of the Nova Scotia fishery, the number of cod living on the Scotia Shelf has plummeted by 96 percent.

Number of Nova Scotians engaged in fishing as their primary occupation in 1880: 29,976
- In 1901: 23,974
- In 1951: 15,607
- In 2002: 7,500

Did you know...

That in the 1920s and 1930s Nova Scotia was the world's largest producer of apples, but with the onset of World War II, the province lost its European market.

NOVA SCOTIA PLACE NAMES

Then:	Now:
Ile Royal	Cape Breton Island
Le Chadye	Cheticamp
St. Charles des Mines	Grand-Pré
St. Famille Parish	Falmouth
Les Mines	Horton

GETTING AROUND

Just a century ago, horse and carriage, trains and boats were the main means by which Nova Scotians travelled their province. The introduction of the automobile, like it did elsewhere, changed forever the way Nova Scotians travelled and how they viewed their home province.

Date on which the "horseless carriage" made its debut in Nova Scotia: September 11, 1899. Curious Nova Scotians came to their doors to watch the noisy machines pass, and many a startled horse was soothed by its rider.

- Year in which the first car was sold: 1904
- Cost per liter of filling up a car in 1904: 10.3 cents
- Number of cars in Nova Scotia in 1916 and 1956: 3,050 and 157,544

The first Nova Scotia motor vehicle law went into effect on April 28, 1907. It required the registration of motor vehicles and cost a one-time fee of $5. The first plate was issued to William Black of Wolfville. Sixty-two other cars were registered that year. Number thirteen was not issued.

In 1923, the rules of Nova Scotia roads changed. Prior to this time, Nova Scotia drivers drove on the left side the road. The new rules mandated right-handed driving.

Today, of course, cars are ubiquitous in Nova Scotia. There are 544,275 cars, motorcycles and busses registered in the province. These travel the more than 23,000 km of road and across 3,900 bridges managed by the Department of Transportation and Public Works.

ELECTRICITY

Life for Nova Scotians was revolutionized in 1884 when electricity was first introduced to Nova Scotians. The first to benefit were Haligonians, when 75 street lights and 50 stores "went electric"

- In 1896, electric street cars were introduced to the province.
- In 1919, the provincial Nova Scotia Power Commission was created.

Today, plugged-in Nova Scotians take electricity for granted, But on September 29, 2003, Nova Scotians were reminded of what life was like before 1884 when Hurricane Juan struck, disrupting power for 300,000 Nova Scotians, some for nearly two weeks. In repairing the damage, power crews replaced 275 transformers, 760 power poles and 125,000 meters of conductor wire.

THEN COMES MARRIAGE

In Nova Scotia, weddings were traditionally community celebrations, planned for months. Community women worked together making quilts, linens and rugs for the couple and the wedding cake (a fruit cake) was made months in advance in order to properly "age" for the big day. The bride in a white gown, and groom in his best suit, were sometimes married in a church, but just as often at home in the family parlour.

After a honeymoon, the couple were welcomed home with a shivaree. Crowds would gather outside the newlyweds' home, making as much noise as possible until they were invited in for tea and cake. Today, marriages continue to be celebrated by friends and family, but with some modern twists. Hosting a wedding can cost the modern couple tens of thousands of dollars; the marriage license alone costs $100 while a courthouse wedding will run a new couple $75 plus tax.

Did you know...

That in 1901 Nova Scotia became the first province in Canada to manufacture cars.

Lunenburg

Old Town Lunenburg was added to the United Nations Educational, Scientific and Cultural Organization World Heritage List in 1995. It is only the second urban community in Continental North America to be included on this list. (The other is old Quebec City.)

Lunenburg received its designation because the Old Town is an outstanding example of British colonial settlement in North America, both in terms of its conception as a model town plan and for its remarkable level of conservation. Thankfully, Lunenburgers were just too practical to tear down buildings that were in perfectly good shape and replace them with the latest designs.

The town still adheres closely to the grid laid down by colonial planners in the 1750s, and more than half of the buildings downtown date back to the 19th century. Lunenburg homes have a widow's walk on the roof, a feature found in many seaports along the East Coast. The most peculiar feature of homes in Lunenburg, and for that matter Lunenburg County, is what is called the "Lunenburg Bump."

The "Bump" is essentially a four or five-sided dormer that overhangs the front (and sometimes back) of the house. They are delightfully diverse, almost as if there was a competition and no neighbour wanted to be accused of imitation.

If you visit Lunenburg, don't confine yourself to just homes and the waterfront. The town has other architectural gems. The Lunenburg Academy (still a working school) is mistaken by many visiting children as a castle, and at night, lit as it often is by lights and the moon, you can understand why.

Although a 2001 fire claimed much of the two-and-a-half-century-old St. John's Anglican Church, it has now been completely rebuilt, standing again as the spiritual and architectural anchor of the Town. St. John's is Canada's second oldest Protestant church and is one of the country's most outstanding examples of the Carpenter Gothic architectural style, the most dominant feature of which is that instead of rendering traditional elements of the church in stone, they are interpreted in wood.

HOUSEHOLD SIZE IN NOVA SCOTIA

1 Person	2 Person
1991: 67,115	1991: 101,415
2001: 89,095	2001: 126,005

4-5 Person	6 + Person
1991: 83, 935	1991: 10, 220
2001: 74, 900	2001: 7,225

GAELIC

At the turn of the twentieth century there were an estimated 100,000 Nova Scotians who spoke Gaelic. After a century of forced assimilation and the growth of mass communication, Gaelic has nearly became a lost language; today just 500 Nova Scotians speak it. There has been a resurgence, however, due in large part to Gaelic language programs offered at Cape Breton's Gaelic College of Celtic Arts and Crafts.

LES ACADIENS

Next to the Mi'kmaq, the Acadians are the oldest inhabitants of Nova Scotia. The Acadians flourished from the outset and, quite amazingly, by 1750 their population reached 10,000, almost solely the result of natural increase. The deportation of the Acadians in 1755 disrupted Nova Scotia's Acadian society, but it did not destroy it.

Beginning in 1764, exiled Acadians returned to l'Acadie, and in the nineteenth century their numbers grew to 45,000. After years of being banned from public life, in 1836 the first two Acadians were named to the Nova Scotia assembly. A nineteenth century rejuvenation of Acadian culture was marked in 1881 by the naming of Acadian national symbols, including the Tricolour flag, a patron saint (Our Lady of the Assumption), and an August 15th national holiday (Assumption Day).

In 2004, Acadians gathered in the province for the Congrès mondial acadien, a celebration of the 400th anniversary of the arrival of the first French speaking settlers in Canada. In 2005, Acadians commemorated the 250th anniversary of the deportation.

HALIFAX NIGHT LIFE

Halifax, the capital city of Nova Scotia, has been and remains a city known for its after-hours revelry. In 1749, the year the city was established, the first liquor license in Nova Scotia history was issued to John Shippey's tavern, The Spread Eagle. By 1760, an estimated 100 pubs provided refreshment in the young city.

Little has changed. Halifax is still reputed to have the highest number of bars per capita than any other city in Canada, and the old Spread Eagle is still open for business, now known as The Split Crow.

The Bluenose

In 1920, The Halifax Herald newspaper sponsored the International Fishing Series, a race between working sailing ships. In the inaugural running, Nova Scotia was defeated and a New England vessel sailed home with the prize. In response to this disappointment, Nova Scotians hired a Halifax designer to build a Nova Scotian ship to contend for the prize

The result was the schooner, the Bluenose, built in Lunenburg by Smith and Rhuland and launched on March 26, 1921. Captained by Lunenburg native Angus Walters, the Bluenose won every race in the International Fishing series from 1921 until 1938.

In 1929, the schooner was featured on the 50-cent stamp. In 1933, it represented the Maritime Provinces at the World's Fair in Chicago, and in 1935 the vessel attended the Silver Jubilee of King George V. Two years later, the image of the Bluenose was added to the dime. World War II, however, forever changed the sailing world, as wooden ships were being replaced with steel hulled vessels.

The 1938 sailing of the International Fishing Series would be the last. When the series was discontinued, Captain Walters fought to save the schooner, buying it himself to prevent its sale at auction. Four years later, however, she was sold to the West Indies Trading Company as a freighter. In January 1946, the Bluenose struck a reef off Haiti and sank.

Economy

INCOME
- Per capita income in 2004: $27,092
- The average annual family income: $51,400
- Canadian average after tax income for a family of two or more people: $60,500
- Average weekly paycheck in Nova Scotia: $597
- Percentage of Nova Scotians who earned less than $5000 in 2002: 16.2
- Percentage who earned more than $60,000: 9

MINIMUM WAGE
- Minimum wage for experienced workers: $6.50
- For inexperienced workers: $6.05

DEBT
Collectively Nova Scotians owe $9.675 billion.
- 65.2 percent of debt is owed on mortgages
- 12.1 percent on vehicle loans
- 7.2 percent on lines of credit
- 6 percent on student loans
- 4.7 percent on credit cards.

Did you know...

That when Nova Scotia joined Confederation in 1867 it was the
wealthiest province in Canada.

TAXES

Provincial sales tax: 8 percent; the combined provincial sales tax and
federal GST is 15 percent.

- Personal income tax rates in Nova Scotia: 8.79 percent to 17.5 percent
- General tax rate: 16 percent
- Small business corporate tax rate: 5 percent

Nova Scotians pay a tax of 15.5 cents/liter of gas – only residents of
Newfoundland pay more.

EMPLOYMENT

- The percentage of Nova Scotians who work is 57.3 percent.
- Percentage of men: 61.7
- Percentage of women: 53.2

Take 5 TOP FIVE THINGS NOVA SCOTIA HOUSEHOLDS SPEND THEIR MONEY ON (AMOUNT SPENT PER YEAR)

1. Personal income taxes ($10,061)
2. Shelter ($9,387)
3. Transportation ($8,099)
4. Food ($6,137)
5. Personal insurance and pension contributions ($3,457)

THE BIG THREE

The three largest employers in the province, each of which employs 5,000 people or more, are the Government of Canada, the Government of Nova Scotia and the Capital District Health Authority.

WOMEN AND THE WORKFORCE

- Women are the sole earners in 11 percent of Nova Scotian families.
- Women working full-time in Nova Scotia earn 71.6 cents for every dollar earned by men working full-time.
- The average annual income of full-time male workers was $40,155 compared to $28,822 for female workers.

THE FOOTPRINT

The average Canadian ecological footprint — the number of hectares of natural resources it takes to sustain the current living standards is 9.86. Number in:

Sudbury: 6.87
Toronto: 7.36
Halifax: 7.83
Calgary: 9.86

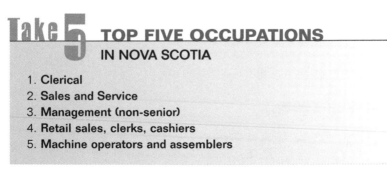

Take 5 TOP FIVE OCCUPATIONS
IN NOVA SCOTIA

1. Clerical
2. Sales and Service
3. Management (non-senior)
4. Retail sales, clerks, cashiers
5. Machine operators and assemblers

WHERE WE WORK

- The median distance of Nova Scotians from their work place is 7.8 kilometers.
- 75 percent drive their own vehicles to work, 9.6 percent carpool, 8 percent walk, 5 percent take public transit.
- Percentage of Nova Scotians who work at home: 10
- Percentage who work a standard 35-40 hour week: 57
- Percentage who work more than 50 hours a week: 16.4

UNEMPLOYMENT

- The unemployment rate in Nova Scotia stands at 9.3 percent.
- The unemployment rate in Halifax Metro, the lowest in the province: 6.7 percent
- The unemployment rate in Cape Breton, the highest: 16.2 percent
- August has the highest rate of unemployment and April the lowest.

SMALL BUSINESS

Thirty-one percent of the Nova Scotia workforce works for a small business with fewer than 50 employees, according to the Canadian Federation of Independent Business.

- Percentage of small businesses that start from scratch: 58
- Percentage that start with the purchase of an existing business: 22
- Percentage that start as the result of taking over a family business: 15
- Percentage that are spin-offs of other businesses: 4
- Percentage located in towns and villages: 38
- Percentage in rural Nova Scotia: 26
- Percentage located in downtown urban areas: 20
- Percentage located in the suburbs: 16

Did you know...

That for every dollar of manufacturing output, Nova Scotia generates $3.39 economic activity.

Bio ROY JODREY

Roy A. Jodrey belongs to the familiar group of early Nova Scotia entrepreneurs who raised themselves up by their bootstraps, compensating for their lack of education with sheer determination and street smarts.

Before Jodrey left school at the age of 12 in Hantsport, Annapolis County, legend now has it that he'd already started two business ventures (he built himself his own water mill to make and sell apple cider and sold blueberries door-to-door). When he left school it didn't mean the end of learning of course. He devoured books on farming, finance, and hydropower, all of which would play a crucial role in business ventures in the future.

By 16, Jodrey was working in his father's apple orchard; by 18, he'd transformed his father's business, shipping apples to new markets in New England. Still in his twenties, Jodrey built a water dam that would produce power for the Annapolis Valley. When he felt power consumption had lagged expectation, he sold electrical appliances.

Scotia Investments

Other dams and a power company would be followed by businesses as diverse as paper, food processing, manufacturing, flower, transportation, real estate development, environmental and waste treatment, metal finishing, specialized coatings and health care. In 1945, Jodrey formed Scotia Investments Limited, an investment holding company to manage the company's interests.

The Jodrey family is by far the richest of all Nova Scotia families. Estimates of the wealth vary but it is believed to be around $340 million, versus, say, the Sobey family, which is estimated to be worth in the neighbourhood of $180 million.

When Roy Jodrey died at the age of 84 in 1973, the 12-year-old boy who had left school was paid this compliment by one of Canada's most skilled corporate lawyers, Frank Covert: "I was associated with Roy Jodrey for 43 years. I know of no man who taught me so much; I know of no man who contributed so much to Nova Scotia, and I know of no man who had higher principles in his dealings with people. He was a man whose word was as good as his bond."

Did you know...

That Nova Scotian households spend an average of $3,119 per year on entertainment and recreation.

SELF-EMPLOYMENT

56,200 Nova Scotians are self-employed. A survey by NovaKnowledge shows that 60 percent of Nova Scotians are willing to take the risk to start their own business.

- Percentage who feel that small businesses are extremely important to the provincial economy: 63
- Percentage who think that running a small business is easy: 35

CAN YOU SAY DOUBLE DOUBLE

- Year in which Ron Joyce, co-founder of Canada's coffee chain, Tim Horton's, was born in Tatamagouche: 1930
- Year in which Joyce and Tim Horton teamed up to market doughnuts: 1965
- Year in which the two became equal partners: 1967
- Date on which Tim Horton was tragically killed in a car crash: 21 February 1974
- Year in which Wendy's and Tim Hortons merged in a $425 million deal, making Ron Joyce the largest shareholder in the American hamburger chain: 1995

Take 5 TOP FIVE INDUSTRIES IN NOVA SCOTIA
(PERCENTAGE OF GDP)

1. **Finance, insurance, real estate and leasing**: 21.5 percent
2. **Manufacturing:** 10.9 percent
3. **Public administration:** 10.2 percent
4. **Health and social sciences:** 7.7 percent
5. **Retail trade:** 6.5 percent

GDP
In 2004, Nova Scotia's GDP stood at $30.036 billion, and accounted for 2.4 percent of Canada's GDP.

ECONOMIC SECTORS (AS PERCENTAGES OF GDP)
- Services production: 75.4
- Private sector: 52.1
- Public sector: 23.3
- Goods production: 24.6
- Primary industry: 7.6
- Secondary industry: 16.9

EXPORTS
Total value of international exports: $5.5 billion

2004 REVENUES OF ATLANTIC CANADA'S FOUR LARGEST COMPANIES
1. Empire Company Limited: $10.6 billion
2. McCain Foods: $6.5 billion
3. Aliant: $2.1 billion
4. Emera: $1.2 billion

Take 5 TOP FIVE INTERNATIONAL EXPORTS
1. Non-metallic minerals, mineral fuels
2. Fish and fish products
3. Plastic and rubber products, excluding tires
4. Paper and paperboard
5. Transportation equipment

FISHING

Fishing typically contributes $340 million to Nova Scotia's GDP.

- Value of international exports of fish and fish products in 2003: $1.18 billion
- Number of full-time jobs (or the equivalent) created by the fishery in Nova Scotia: 7,500
- Average income generated by this industry: $25,000

Nova Scotians harvest 30 species of fish.

- Number of boats that fish, according to the latest Department of Fisheries data: 5,452
- Of these, the number of boats that fish the inshore: 5,350

LOBSTER

Nova Scotia is the world's top exporter of lobster. The crustacean is Canada's number one seafood export and is consumed in 55 nations.

- The average cost of a lobster fishing license (which includes license, boat and gear): $100,000 to $200,000

OVER-POPULATION

Ratio of commercial sized lobster off the coast of Nova Scotia to the actual people population of the province: 85:1

- Average number of eggs a single female lobster carries: up to 20,000

Take 5 — TOP FIVE SHELLFISH/ CRUSTACEAN EXPORTS

1. **Lobster:** $442 million
2. **Crab:** $154 million
3. **Scallops:** $131 million
4. **Shrimp:** $110 million
5. **Clams:** $55 million

Did you know...

- That the largest recorded lobster was caught off southern Nova Scotia in 1977? It weighed in at 44 lb. 6 oz. and measured 3 ft. 6 in. from the end of the tail to the tip of the largest claw.

- That only 35 years ago lobster was not a delicacy at all, but rather it was considered a "poor man's food," a common and mundane meal that children unhappily carried in their school lunches.

ANATOMY OF A DELICACY

For every 100 g of steamed lobster there are 98 calories, 20.47 g of protein, 0.6 g of fat, 72 mg cholesterol, 1.3 g carbohydrates, 1.6 g minerals, 380 mg sodium, 352 mg potassium and 61 mg calcium.

FISH FARMING

There are approximately 400 aquaculture sites in Nova Scotia and together they produce 7.9 million kilograms of fish worth $40 million.

FISH PROCESSING

There are 295 licensed fish processing plants in Nova Scotia and together they contribute more than $300 million to the provincial GDP. More than 7,300 people work in the plants, and plants export more than $690 million in processed goods.

Take 5 TOP FIVE FINFISH EXPORTS

1. **Cod:** $72 million
2. **Haddock:** $48 million
3. **Perch:** $48 million
4. **Groundfish:** $36 million
5. **Herring:** $35 million

Bluefin

The magnificent Atlantic bluefin tuna was not always held in the esteem it is today. Until the 1930s, it was considered a nuisance fish, preying on the much more valuable cod and herring stocks. In Nova Scotia, if they were caught at all it was to eliminate their effect on the other fisheries. They literally sold for pennies to cat food manufactures, or were ploughed into the soil for fertilizer.

Today, even non-fishers' eyes alight at the word bluefin. And why wouldn't they? Even if it didn't make it to the world's trendy sushi restaurants, its sheer size and speed would guarantee it public interest. It is the world's largest bony fish, reaching over half a ton in weight, and today fetching more than $150,000 a fish. It has been known to dive to depths of up to 500 meters and is an inveterate traveller. Tagged bluefin have been tracked swimming 7,500 kilometers across the Atlantic in 119 days, meaning if they were swimming in a straight line they would be putting in 65 km a day.

It was the Americans who first flocked to the small Nova Scotia fishing village of Wedgeport to pursue the ultimate trophy fish that ultimately alerted the local population to its potential value. People like Ernest Hemingway, business magnate Michael Lerner, Amelia Earhart, Kate Smith and Franklin D. Roosevelt all came in pursuit of the big game fish.

Atlantic bluefin landed in Nova Scotia are still famous, only now they are eaten by humans rather than cats. From June through October, the period when they are off the Nova Scotia coast, they can increase their body mass by 40 percent. A Nova Scotian, Ken Fraser, holds the world record for the largest bluefin catch, a 1,496-pounder he hooked on October 26th, 1979 off Auld's Cove.

BLUEFIN

Nova Scotia is well known for the bluefin tuna stocks off its coast. Over the years, this fish has had many nicknames. In the nineteenth century, Bluenosers called them "horse mackerel" and in the twentieth century, "sea lions."

MANUFACTURING

Approximately ten percent of the Nova Scotia economy is accounted for by manufacturing. The value of the goods manufactured and exported annually is approaching $9 billion and the manufacturing sector grew 26 percent faster than the economy as a whole between 1990 and 2003.

- 11 percent of employed Nova Scotians work in manufacturing.
- Nova Scotia's exports of province-manufactured goods grew by 95.8 percent between 1990 and 2003. These goods accounted for half of all Nova Scotia exports.
- The top three manufacturing industries in Nova Scotia are food industries, refined petroleum/coal industries and transportation equipment industries.

TIRES

On October 3, 2000, Michelin North America's three Nova Scotian plants at Bridgewater, Granton and Waterville produced its 150 millionth tire.

- The first 50 million took the company 15 years to produce.
- The second 50 million took eight years.
- The last 50 million just five years.
- Almost 3,500 Nova Scotians work for Michelin.

Did you know...

Fishing was the most dangerous industry in Nova Scotia for on-the-job injuries in 2004.

MINING

Nova Scotia's mining industry is worth just over $270 million to the Nova Scotia economy and 1,431 Nova Scotians work in the mining industry.

- Over 6.96 million tonnes of gypsum is shipped from the province annually. This accounts for 83 percent of all gypsum mined in Canada.
- 374,000 tonnes of coal are exported.
- 13.2 tonnes of crushed stone, sand and gravel leave the province.
- We Did It First: First Coal Mines in Canada.
- In 1720, Canada's first coal mine was opened in Cape Breton.

GOLD IN THEM THAR HILLS

Gold mining is embedded deep in Nova Scotia's history, with first sightings of the ore being made as early as 1578. In the 1830s, labourers building roads discovered a "bright yellow metal" in the stone. In 1851, the first authenticated gold find was made at Mooseland, and nine years later, John Gerrish Pulsiver found more at that site. The gold rush was on.

Other gold districts followed and overnight, towns sprung up filled with speculators looking to get rich quick. In 1867, Nova Scotia mined 27,538 ounces, the most gold to that date ever to be taken from the province. The rush, marred by poor methods and incompetence, was short.

Thanks to improved technology, by the turn of the century the industry was revived and in 1898, 31,113 ounces were mined. By this time, however, the Klondike Rush was in full swing, and would-be miners left Nova Scotia, hoping to strike it even richer out west. There was still life in the Nova Scotia gold mines, though. The 1920s and 1930s and the early 1950s would see gold fever strike for the third and fourth times.

Did you know...

That Nova Scotia is home to an estimated 3 billion tonnes of coal.

OFFSHORE OIL AND GAS

The offshore oil industry contributes more than $1 billion to the Nova Scotia GDP every year.

- Year in which Mobil Oil Canada received the first offshore license to explore for gas off Nova Scotia, in the Sable Island block: 1959
- Year Mobil Oil started to drill: 1967
- Number of wells that had been drilled off Nova Scotia by 2001: 140
- Number of these that resulted in significant discoveries: 22

Gas started flowing from the Sable Offshore Energy Project Five in 1999.

- Average number of cubic feet of natural gas produced every day: 400 million
- Number of barrels of natural gas liquids produced every day: 20,000

FORESTRY AND LOGGING

- Two million cords of wood are harvested annually in Nova Scotia.
- Nova Scotia exports more than $1.1 billion worth of forest products annually.

- Rank of Nova Scotia as a Canadian producer of pulp and paper: 5
- Number of Nova Scotians working in jobs directly related to the forestry industry: 11,900
- Percentage of Nova Scotia's forest products accounted for by newspaper: 28
- Other paper and paperboard: 28 percent
- Wood pulp: 20
- Softwood lumber: 18
- Other products: 6

Did you know...

That Nova Scotia maple trees yield more than 118,182 liters of maple syrup each year.

Did you know...

That Nova Scotia is the world's largest exporter of lobsters, Christmas trees, gypsum, carrots, wild blueberries, strawberry plants and fur.

The top three export markets for forestry products are:
- USA (72 percent)
- South and Central America (12 percent)
- European Union (6 percent).

OH CHRISTMAS TREES
More than 2,500 people grow Christmas trees in Nova Scotia, farming 9,490 hectares of land. Each year, nearly two million trees are sent to market.

SELLING CANADA'S OCEAN PLAYGROUND
In 2003, tourism injected $ 1.27 billion into the provincial economy.
- Number of people who visited Nova Scotia in 2004: 2.24 million
- Percentage who came from elsewhere in Canada: 84
- Number of Atlantic Canadians who visited the province, accounting for 55 percent of all visitors: 1.23 million
- Percentage from the United States: 14
- Percentage from overseas: 3

Take 5 TOP FIVE CONTAINER IMPORTS
TO THE PORT OF HALIFAX

1. **Machinery – machinery, mechanical appliances, parts**
2. **Building – other ceramic products**
3. **Chemicals – other inorganic**
4. **Miscellaneous manufactured goods**
5. **Furniture/lights/mattresses**

Did you know...

That Sobeys is the only Nova Scotia business that numbers in
the top 50 largest employers in Canada.

PORT OF HALIFAX

Halifax's deep, ice-free harbour makes it one of the most valuable in
the country and a boon to the province's economy.

* Each year the port generates almost $700 million.
* More than 9,000 Nova Scotians work directly and indirectly for the
  port of Halifax.

CARS

In 2003, 46,630 new cars were bought in Nova Scotia, contributing
$1.3 billion to the province in sales.

AGRICULTURE

The combined farm gate value of Nova Scotian-grown agricultural products is more than $420 million annually. More than 9,000 Nova Scotians
are directly employed by agriculture and around ten percent of Nova
Scotia's workforce is somehow connected to the agri-food industry.

Take 5 TOP FIVE CONTAINER EXPORTS
FROM THE PORT OF HALIFAX

1. **Newsprint**
2. **Machinery/mechanical appliances/parts**
3. **Wood/wood pulp**
4. **Vegetables**
5. **Paper**

They Said It

HOW MUCH?

Farmers in Nova Scotia produce:

- 36,000 beef cattle
- 226,000 hogs
- 33 million kilograms of chicken
- 18 million dozen eggs
- 173,000 kilolitres of milk
- 2 million bushels of apples
- 18 million kg of wild blueberries
- 91 million kg of fresh vegetables.

WE DID IT FIRST

North America's first Agricultural Fair was held in Windsor, Nova Scotia, in 1752.

FARM COUNTRY

According to the latest Statistics Canada data, Nova Scotia has 3,923 farms, occupying some 407,047 hectares of land.

Nine percent have fewer than four hectares, while 0.9 percent have 650 hectares or more.

Did you know...

- That every year Nova Scotia sends the city of Boston a large Christmas tree, a thank-you for aid Bostonians provided to an explosion-ravished Halifax in 1917.
- That Nova Scotia was home to Canada's first decorated Christmas tree, in 1846.

HIGH TECH FARMING

Almost 40 percent of Nova Scotian farms use computers on the farm.

DAIRY INDUSTRY

Of the 3,923 farms in Nova Scotia, 1,705 have dairy cows. There are approximately 108,000 cows in the province, 24,000 of which are dairy cows. Milk and cream sales alone fetch almost $100 million annually.

Bio FRANK SOBEY

He was born Frank Hoyse Sobey in 1902 at Lyons Brook in Pictou County. By the time young Frank was three, his father left the family farm for Stellarton to start a butchering business.

Young Frank was not a good student and disliked school. At 16, having completed just grade eight, he left school completely, eventually joining his father in the butchering business. In 1924, on the advice of young Frank, the Sobey's meat business expanded, and non-meat groceries were added to the store's shelves.

When young Frank and his new bride, Irene McDonald, and her family travelled to Boston, a new era for the Sobey business had effectively begun. While the rest of the entourage toured the historic city, Frank toured grocery stores, getting from them the ideas that he would implement when he returned home.

Like the New England stores he visited, he decided to open a store based not on credit, but rather a cash and carry supermarket. By the early 1930s, that formula allowed him to open six stores across western Nova Scotia. By the mid-1940s, Frank was elected mayor of Stellarton and he had opened his 25th store.

Frank Sobey continued to expand his supermarket chain through the twentieth century. When he died in 1987, company sales exceeded $1 billion for the first time. Today, the company has more than 1,200 stores and $5 billion in annual sales.

TOP FIVE TOURISM-DOLLAR GENERATING REGIONS
IN NOVA SCOTIA

1. **Halifax-Dartmouth:** $620 million
2. **Cape Breton:** $212 million
3. **Annapolis Valley:** $163 million
4. **South Shore:** $102 million
5. **Fundy Shore:** $86 million

FRUITS AND VEGETABLES

- 1,085 Nova Scotian farms grow fruit.
- 695 grow blueberries
- 272 grow apples
- 132 grow strawberries
- 404 grow vegetables
- 118 grow carrots
- 139 grow green or waxed beans
- 106 grow green peas

Nova Scotia produced 40,000 tonnes of apples, 1.58 million kilograms of strawberries and 26.4 million kg of blueberries.

WILD BERRIES

Nova Scotia is the world's top exporter of wild berries. This crop is sold in markets in the U.S., Germany, Japan, France, United Kingdom, Scandinavia, Italy, Netherlands, Switzerland, Taiwan, Caribbean, and Australia.

- In 2004, 15,067 hectares of wild blueberries were grown in Nova Scotia.
- 17.5 million kg of blueberries were grown, worth more than $20,050,000 to farmers.

Did you know...

That in Nova Scotia, dairy cows produce 1,863,000 glasses of milk a day.

Take 5 TOP FIVE MONTHS FOR NEW AUTO SALES IN NOVA SCOTIA

1. **May** (6,021 units purchased)
2. **July** (4,853)
3. **April** (4,826)
4. **June** (4,461)
5. **August** (4,047)

EGG INDUSTRY

Nova Scotia farms have more than 717,000 laying chickens. They produce more than 17.2 million dozen eggs, hatching a tidy $ 21 million annually.

GRAPE GROWING

Despite its cool climate, Nova Scotia is home to a number of successful vineyards. In 1982, the Grape Growers Association of Nova Scotia was established. Today, 22 grape growers work 160 hectares of grape vines. The most widely planted white wine grape is L'Acadie, while the main red wine grape is the Maréchal Foch.

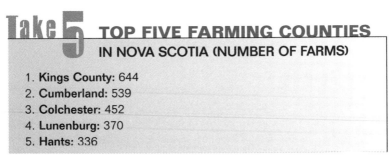

Take 5 TOP FIVE FARMING COUNTIES IN NOVA SCOTIA (NUMBER OF FARMS)

1. **Kings County:** 644
2. **Cumberland:** 539
3. **Colchester:** 452
4. **Lunenburg:** 370
5. **Hants:** 336

Did you know...

WINE MAKING

Nova Scotia has a number of winemaking operations. The Annapolis Valley, the warmest, driest, region, is home to the first Nova Scotia winery, the Grand Pré Winery (now called Domaine de Grand Pré), which opened in the 1970s. Two one-time growers for the Grand Pré Winery, Sainte Famille and Blomidon Estate, are now themselves bona fide wine making operations. Along the Northumberland shore, the Jost family opened their winery in 1983, and they have since been joined by Lunenburg County Winery, Petite Rivière Vineyards & Winery and Gaspereau Vineyards.

Together these wineries make, 59 wines – 26 white, 23 red, two rosé, one fortified, and seven dessert/late harvest wines. A number of these vineyards and wineries offer tours of their vineyards and production facilities and sell their products directly to the public on site.

MAKING MOVIES IN "HOLLYWOOD EAST"

- In the past six years, Nova Scotia's film production industry has netted $100 million and employs 2,000 Nova Scotians.
- In 2004, 39 film and television projects were made in Nova Scotia. This same year, 40 Nova Scotia-made films were nominated for Gemini Awards, with 18 winning the coveted prize.

They Said It

"It's going to be a lot of bleeps."
– Mike Volpe, executive producer of the hit Nova Scotia-made comedy series, The Trailer Park Boys, commenting on the 2005-2006 season

Bio ALEXANDER KEITH

Popular lore portrays Alexander Keith as the affable Haligonian who brought Nova Scotians their favorite beer. Television commercials take it a bit further, portraying him as a man who loved a good folk song and had a penchant for pretty bar wenches. The question is, who was the real Alexander Keith?

He was born in Scotland in October 1795, and as a teenager his father sent him to England to learn the brewing trade. At the age of 22, he immigrated to Halifax, where he worked for brewmaster Charles Boggs. By 1820, Keith bought out Boggs and began his career as a brewer. In 1822, he moved his business to Water Street, building Keith Hall in 1863.

Alexander Keith was very involved in the life of his booming young city, serving on various boards and associations. He was especially involved in the Freemasons, becoming a provincial Grand Master. In 1841, he was elected to city council, serving as mayor in 1853, and 1854. In 1843 he was appointed to the Nova Scotia Legislative Council, and at Confederation in 1867, pro-confederate Keith was offered, but declined, an appointment to the Canadian Senate.

Alexander Keith's life was not without controversy. During the American Civil War, many Haligonians, Keith among them, favored the cause of Southerners. Reportedly, Keith, on more than one occasion, helped Southern raiders escape capture off the northeast coast. Though unproven, it has been suggested that Keith was in fact a spy for the South. When Keith died in Halifax in December 1873, his estate was valued at $251,000.

Crime and Punishment

CRIME LINE

August 26, 1749	First murder in Halifax.
August 31, 1749	Canada's first ever trial under British Law, at Halifax.
January 1, 1835	Joseph Howe publishes his famous letter and is charged with Libel.
March 1835	After defending himself, Howe acquitted.
July 30 1844	The mutinous, murderous crew of the Saladin hanged publicly.
December 1923	J.B. McLachlan charged with sedition, sentenced to two years.
December 15, 1937	In Nova Scotia's last execution, Everett Farmer is hanged for murder.
February 12, 1964	Lutz triple murder.
November 1971	Donald Marshall Jr. wrongly accused of murder.
February 7, 1990	The province officially apologizes to Donald Marshall Jr.
May 27, 1990	Largest hashish seizure in Canadian history, at Ragged Harbour, Nova Scotia.
May 7, 1992	Triple killing at the Sydney McDonald's restaurant. Crime Stoppers program initiated in Nova Scotia.

2002	Clayton Johnson, wrongfully convicted for the 1993 murder of his wife, has his conviction overturned and is freed.
2004	Nova Scotia Supreme Court celebrates its 250th birthday.
2005	Statistics Canada reveals that Nova Scotia has the 8th highest crime rate in the nation.
June 2005	Nova Scotia Crime Stoppers reports that since its inception, the program has resulted in 60,571 calls to its hotline, 4580 laid charges, $3,303,310 in recovered stolen property and $4,954,284 worth of illicit drugs seized.
August 2005	Nova Scotians are shocked when two affable young men from the peaceful community of Glen Haven are discovered murdered.

WE DID IT FIRST: CANADA'S FIRST TRIAL FOR MURDER

Peter Cartcel has the dubious distinction of being the first Halifax murderer charged and tried for his crime. On August 26th, 1749, Cartcel fatally stabbed Abraham Goodsides as the two fought on the streets of the infant city. Because Nova Scotia had no court system, the murder required Gov. Edward Cornwallis to take immediate action.

Empowered to establish courts for the fledging city, Cornwallis named himself and six councillors to the city's first court. On the

They Said It

"*A hanging day . . . brings the worst of Halifax to the market place. They press against the gallows, their eyes eager. A fiendish festivity marks the occasion. They cheer at the launching and persist in mocking the hanged-man until his final gasp.*"
— **The fictional character "Fetch," Robert E. Kroll (ed). Intimate Fragments: An Irreverent Chronicle of Early Halifax.**

31st of August, Cartcel appeared without a lawyer before the hastily established court for Canada's first ever trial under British law. After hearing four witnesses, the court deliberated for just half an hour before they found the defendant guilty. Two days later, Cartcel was hanged.

NO BETTER WAY TO SPEND A
SATURDAY WITH THE KIDDIES

Nova Scotians found guilty of capital crimes in the 18th, 19th and even the early 20th centuries faced death by hanging. In 1785 alone, 12 people were hanged, one of those charged with stealing potatoes! Entertainment-starved Haligonians eagerly staked out the best vantage point from which to view hangings, which were often held in public spots such as the market or on the Commons.

MURDEROUS MUTINIES

In May of 1844, the ship Saladin ran aground on Nova Scotia's eastern shore. The claims of the small crew of six was that the captain and other crew members had died at sea raised immediate suspicions. The crew was placed under arrest, and charged with killing their captain and five crew mates.

As confessions were elicited, a grizzly story of mutiny and murder took shape. The ringleader, George Fielding (this former captain had been in prison prior to the journey, but made a deal with authorities to work the trip for free passage for himself and his 14 year-old son), had convinced four crewmen to help him carry out his dastardly deed. On April 14, 1844, they used axes and other tools on board to kill the captain and five mates. When his compatriots learned of Fielding's plans to sweeten his own share of the loot through further killings, they turned on him, throwing him and his son overboard.

After only 15 minutes of deliberation, the jury returned guilty verdicts in three cases. Two of the men, tried separately, were acquitted. The convicted pirates were hanged on July 30, 1844. Hundreds of

Haligonians brought their families to witness the event on the South Common, the site today of the old Victoria General Hospital.

END OF AN ERA
Everett Farmer, a Nova Scotian labourer charged with murdering his brother-in-law, was the last person to be hanged in the province. As a poor, black, Shelburne County man, Farmer had access to legal counsel of dubious quality. Farmer insisted that his crime had been one of self-defence, but without adequate representation it was hard for him to make his case.

A lawyer was not assigned to his defence until just one week before the opening of his September 1937 trial. As the first capital case to be heard in Shelburne County for a century, the Farmer trial became a media circus.

Juried by twelve white men, the trial lasted just two days and ended in a murder conviction. Everett Farmer was sentenced to die. According to a newspaper account, at 5 a.m. on December 15th, Farmer climbed the stairs of the hanging scaffold "with the same coolness that [had] characterized him since he [had] been in jail." As the hood was placed over his head, and as his spiritual advisor recited scripture, Farmer uttered his last words before the trap was sprung, "Good-bye, boys."

GAOL OF GEORGE'S ISLAND
Time in jail at George's Island off the Halifax shore was no island retreat. Like most prisons of the day, Her Majesty's Georges Island

They Said It

"We are all capable of murder … People have their breaking points. … I really do think that when it comes to murder, we're all brothers and sisters, and we could all be murderers in the right circumstances."
— **Donald Clairmont, director of the Atlantic Institute of Criminology**

Gaol of the 1700s and 1800s was the wretched home of rats and rogues and their communicable maladies. For more than a century, errant military men — traitors, mutineers and deserters, as well as unfortunate civilians - were imprisoned on the island while they awaited their fates – exile, flogging, or death by hanging.

OUTLAWING LIQUOR

In the late 19th and early 20th centuries, the use and sale of alcohol was a political and social hot potato. Following a crusade that began in the early nineteenth century, pro-temperance Nova Scotians got their wish when Canada passed the 1878 Canada Temperance Act legislation that allowed all communities to vote on whether or not they would become 'dry.'

Most Nova Scotian municipalities - one exception being Halifax - voted to outlaw drinking. With the Temperance Act of 1910, Nova Scotians were legally allowed to buy alcohol only for "medicinal, sacramental, art, trade and manufacturing purposes." Again, Halifax was the exception; there, people continued to drink, entitled by law.

In 1916, Nova Scotia abandoned the local option approach to prohibition and went stone dry. Alcohol consumption was banned across the province, even in Halifax. For the next 14 years, Nova Scotians could not legally have a drink.

(RUM) RUNNING FROM THE LAW

Out of prohibition sprung a new, lucrative and illegal rum trade. Former temperance inspector enforcement officer and New Glasgow native Clifford Rose recalls that his own sleepy Nova Scotia hamlet contained illegal rum dives that were "thick as bees."

One of the most colourful characters in Rose's memoirs is Delores N., the feisty proprietor of a local watering hole and a woman with an "obscene and profane tongue," a disabled husband and several children to raise.

In one raid on Delores' establishment, the business woman

acquainted the back of Rose's head with a liquor bottle. Recognizing the pervasiveness of the illegal industry, the financial rewards that drove Nova Scotians like Delores to embrace it, and the utter corruption of so-called enforcement officials, a cynical Rose celebrated the 1929 defeat of prohibition in his province.

SMUGGLER'S PARADISE

Nova Scotia is still a haven for smuggling illicit substances, thanks to its sheltered coves and inlets and its isolated, unguarded coastline. In the late 1970s, heightened coastal protection in the United States, coupled with its geography, made Nova Scotia a favoured drop-off spot for drug smugglers. While the entire South Shore has seen a rapid rise in smuggling activity over the past three decades, the remote coasts of Queens and Shelburne Counties have emerged as the biggest 'pipelines' for illegal drug transactions.

In the 1970s, the Coastal Watch Program was initiated at RCMP request. Nova Scotians living near the coast are asked to report suspicious offshore activities. RCMP estimates suggest that 10 percent of the cocaine and 50 percent of the cannabis imported into Canada arrives by water, and a good deal of this comes via Nova Scotia's South Shore.

On May 27th 1990, the largest seizure of hashish in Canadian history went down in Ragged Harbour, Nova Scotia. Thanks to reports furnished by a local lobster fisherman, police were tipped off to a smuggling operation of 25 tonnes of hashish, with an estimated street value of more than $400 million.

In February 1994, Nova Scotian authorities made another huge bust off the rocky shore of Nova Scotia. Two years of RCMP investi-

They Said It

"The business of one half of the town is to sell rum, and the other half to drink it."
— **Rev. Dr. Ezra Stiles, President of Yale College, referring to Halifax.**

gations were rewarded with a massive drug seizure in Shelburne. The vessel, Lady Teri-Anne, was weighed down with 5,419 kilograms of cocaine, worth $1 billion.

MURDER

According to Donald Clairmont, director of the Atlantic Institute of Criminology at Dalhousie University, people kill for three reasons: passion, profit, or inexplicably, for no apparent reason.

In 2003, there were eight homicides in Nova Scotia, 1.5 percent of the total 548 homicides reported to police in Canada in 2003.

Shooting was the most common cause of death in murders. Sixty-six murders in Nova Scotia between 1988 and 1997 involved shooting. Stabbing came second, at 48 incidents, and beatings third, at 28 incidents.

Between 1999 and 2003, there were 54 murders in Nova Scotia. The rate of homicide per 100,000 of the Nova Scotian population is 0.9, much lower than the national rate of 1.7.

MURDERS OF PASSION

Marriage can bring great love and understanding. It can also wreak anger and violence.

Of the 164 murder cases in Nova Scotia between 1988 and 1997, almost half were related to domestic disputes of some sort.

According to the Nova Scotia Advisory Council on the Status of Women, women are twice as likely to suffer homicide at the hand of a spouse than are men.

They Said It

"We're talking about massive amounts. Even today, we still don't have any idea how much is getting through. We do know, though, that the seizures we do make are only a small portion of the total picture."
— Gary Grant, RCMP, on drug smuggling in Nova Scotia

Take 5 DEAN JOBB'S
FIVE MOST DEVIOUS CRIMINALS
IN NOVA SCOTIA

Dean Jobb hunted down Nova Scotia's most intriguing criminals for three books of true-crime stories, including *Shades of Justice*: Seven Nova Scotia Murder Cases, winner of the Evelyn Richardson award for best non-fiction work by a Nova Scotia writer. He is also the author of *The Acadians: A Peoples Story of Exile and Triumph* and *Calculated Risk: Greed, Politics and the Westray Tragedy*. A former reporter, editor and columnist for the Halifax Herald, Dean is an assistant professor of journalism at the University of King's College in Halifax. He lives in Wolfville.

1. **Lt.-Colonel Charles Lawrence**. Nova Scotia's acting governor in 1755, Lawrence was the driving force behind the brutal expulsion of 10,000 Acadian men, women and children from their homeland and their dispersal to the American Colonies, England and France. At least 5,000 deportees died of disease and hunger or drowned in shipwrecks in an act of genocide and ethnic cleansing that ranks Lawrence among the world's most ruthless criminals.

2. **The Saladin Pirates**. They are hardly household names, but Charles Anderson, John Hazelton, George Jones and William Travaskiss committed one of the bloodiest mutinies of the Age of Sail. On a voyage from South America to England in 1844, they rose up against the captain of the cargo ship Saladin and later tossed the ringleader of the mutiny overboard. A shocking tale of the murder of eight men emerged after the ship ran aground on the Eastern Shore. The four were tried, convicted, and publicly hanged on the Halifax Commons.

3. **Samuel Herbert Dougal**. When Dougal, a retired soldier, was convicted of murdering a wealthy heiress in Britain in 1903, Scotland Yard detectives started asking questions about the sudden deaths of

two Halifax women almost two decades earlier. Dougal, a sergeant in the Royal Engineers, was stationed in Halifax in June 1885 when his first wife, Lovenia, died. He remarried Mary Boyd six weeks later but she died that October. Bad luck? Coincidence? The authorities could not rule out the possibility that Dougal had been a serial killer who preyed on women.

4. **Jack Randell**. His motto was "Once a scrapper, always a scrapper," and Newfoundland-born skipper Randell was a scrapper. In March 1929, he was at the wheel of the Lunenburg-based rumrunner *I'm Alone*, trying to land a load of illegal booze in Louisiana, when a U.S. Coast Guard cutter chased his schooner deep into international waters. The cutter opened fire, sending the I'm Alone to the bottom, killing one of Randell's crewmen and sparking a diplomatic row between Canada and the U.S. The Americans later apologized for the breach of international law and compensated Randell for the loss of his boat.

5. **James Forman**. The first cashier of the Bank of Nova Scotia almost turned out to be its last. In 1870, a junior clerk stumbled upon a shortfall in the accounts of the bank, which was founded in Halifax in 1835. It turned out to be the tip of an iceberg – $320,000 was missing, embezzled over the previous 25 years to finance Forman's lavish lifestyle, which included a mansion in the city's fashionable south end. As the size of the fraud became apparent, Forman fled to London to escape prosecution. He died there the following year. The bank, nearly ruined by the loss and the blow to public confidence, soldiered on to become one of Canada's leading financial institutions.

FURY OF A MADMAN

"I've done a terrible thing. I shot four people." This was the chilling confession of Aubrey Lutz, made to officers at the Kentville, N.S. RCMP detachment on February 12th, 1964. Lutz had recently married 18 year-old Rosalie Pudsey.

Rosalie and Aubrey's marriage began to sour, and fearing for her safety, Rosalie took the couples' newborn baby, Kimberly, to live with her parents and two sisters. Rosalie's move enraged Aubrey, and on that fateful day he loaded his gun and went to confront his wife and her family. Aubrey met and killed Rosalie's mother first. When Rosalie's younger sister Audrey sought refuge in the bathroom, Aubrey fired through the door, instantly killing the 15-year-old. On hearing the commotion, Rosalie Lutz climbed the stairs from the basement and placed baby Kimberly on the living room couch. When she confronted her husband, he fired, striking her in the shoulder.

ESCAPE

Just as Aubrey was about to make his escape, Arthur Pudsey returned home to the awful scene. For the fourth time Aubrey fired his gun, this time killing his father-in-law. Aubrey grabbed his unharmed baby and travelled to Kentville where he confessed to police. Rosalie Lutz and her nine-year old sister, who had been at school, were the sole surviving members of their family. Deemed unfit to stand trial, Lutz was sent to the Nova Scotia Hospital. For almost fifteen years he remained a volatile, dangerous man who was heavily medicated and received almost 500 shock treatments.

They Said It

"One of the most dangerous times for a woman (and her children) is when she leaves."
—Former chairwoman of the NS Advisory Council on the Status of Women, Patricia Doyle Bedwell

In the late 1970s and 1980s, however, Lutz's demeanor improved and he was classified a voluntary patient, free to check himself out. On December 27th, 1990, the murderer of three left the Nova Scotia Hospital a free man and returned to his Annapolis Valley home. Horrified, Rosalie called police. Lutz was again arrested, charged with three counts of murder and prepared for trial. In March 1991, the courts made a familiar ruling – Lutz was deemed unfit for trial, and remanded into the custody of the Nova Scotia Hospital, where he remains. Amazingly, Rosalie has forgiven Aubrey: "I believe everyone should leave him alone. I have forgiven my husband for what he has done."

THE KILLINGS AT MCDONALD'S

In the early pre-dawn morning of May 7th, 1992, three young Sydney-area men arrived at the city's McDonald's restaurant intending to commit robbery. Derek Wood, Darren Muise and Freeman MacNeil were sure that the restaurant's safe contained as much as $200,000.

The robbery turned deadly when the three encountered the four staff members on the midnight shift. Armed with knives, a .22 caliber pistol and a shovel, the three robbers brutally murdered Donna Warren, Neil Borroughs and Jimmy Fagan, and left Arlene MacNeil badly wounded and near death.

The horrific crime stunned and outraged the small city, and indeed the whole nation, as national media descended on Sydney. The perpetrators denied their involvement but evidence against them mounted, and by the middle of May all had confessed their crime.

They were variously charged with murder, robbery and the unlawful confinement of Donna Warren, who had been forced to open the safe before she, like the others, was shot in the head. Harsh punishment was meted out to the murderers. Darren Muise was sentenced to life in prison without parole for twenty years and Freeman MacNeil got life in prison with no parole for twenty-five years. Derek Wood was sentenced to two life terms in jail, and ten years for robbery and unlawful confinement.

CRIMES BY THE NUMBER
- 82,116 criminal code incidents were recorded in Nova Scotia in 2004
- 75,479 of the criminal cases involved adults
- 6,637 involved youth

IN 2004, THERE WERE:
- 13 homicides
- 9,121 assaults
- 739 robberies involving violence
- 3,352 motor vehicle thefts
- 20,222 other thefts
- 7,787 break-and-enters
- 820 sexual assaults
- 13,702 mischief cases

AVERAGE JOE OFFENDER
- 20-24 years old
- guilty of property crime
- sentenced 1-3 months

TO SERVE AND PROTECT
There are a total of 1,615 police officers in Nova Scotia, or 172 for every 100,000 citizens.

Nationally, there are 59,906 police officers, or 184 per 100,000 Canadians.

Did you know...

That Nova Scotia has 87 courtrooms.

ELEVEN LOST YEARS

On May 28th, 1971, sixteen-year-old Donald Marshall Jr. was walking through a Sydney park when he met up with Sandy Seale, another youth from Sydney. The two teenagers then encountered Roy Ebsary, described as an "eccentric old man with a fetish for knives." Without warning, Ebsary brutally and fatally stabbed Seale.

Police arrested and charged Marshall, a Mi'kmaq from Membertou, with Seale's death, and in November 1971 Marshall was sentenced to life in prison. For 11 years Marshall was incarcerated; for 11 years he maintained his innocence. In 1982, Marshall was released on bail as then Justice Minister, Jean Chrétien, referred the case to the Nova Scotia Supreme Court for rehearing.

In 1983, Donald Marshall Jr. was acquitted of all charges, but in a strange outcome the police who had wrongly charged him were absolved of all wrongdoing. In a now infamous statement, Chrétien reasoned that any miscarriage of justice was "more apparent than real." Roy Ebsary was eventually convicted of manslaughter in the death of Seale. For eleven lost years of his life, Donald Marshall accepted a lump sum payment of $270,000 from the Nova Scotia government, but was required to pay his own legal bills.

FAKIN' IT

In 2003, there were 4,446 counterfeit bank notes passed and seized by police in Nova Scotia – accounting for about one percent of the 443,303 phony bills that were passed and seized nationwide. Nationally, seized counterfeit notes had a face value of $12,715,010.

CROSSING THE THIN BLUE LINE

In August 2004, Joseph Daniel Ryan, a former Halifax RCMP officer, was found guilty of stealing drugs that had been seized by his Tantallon RCMP detachment. An enterprising Ryan had been selling confiscated drugs to local dealers. Arrested by fellow officers who had been directed to Ryan by an informant, Ryan was sentenced to four years in prison for his crime.

NO COVER UP

On July 13th, 2001, four men and one woman were arrested after police received complaints of public nudity at Crystal Crescent Beach. Although public nudity is illegal in Nova Scotia, such cases need the approval of the Attorney General before they can commence. In this case, the Nova Scotia Attorney General refused to initiate the proceedings, stating, "Citizens should not face a criminal conviction for conduct of this type without aggravating factors, such as aggressive exhibitionism, or lewd or indecent acts. According to the police investigation, none of these aggravating factors was present."

Expulsion of the Acadians

The first French settlers arrived in Acadia, an area consisting of present-day Nova Scotia, New Brunswick, and a part of Québec and Maine, in 1604. By the turn of the next century, there were upwards of 1,500 Acadians, a figure that would jump to almost 15,000 fifty years later.

Although it was the wars in Europe that caused Acadia to pass back and forth between the English and French during the 17th and 18th centuries, the battle in North America was also about numbers. Until the founding of Halifax in 1749, and the subsequent push on the part of the English to promote immigration, the Acadian population outnumbered the English-sponsored immigrants, something of which the colonial government took strong notice.

In 1713, a part of Acadia became Nova Scotia. Rather than leave, the Acadians chose to live under British rule. Asked to take an oath of allegiance to the British Crown, Acadians instead said they would remain neutral or sign a conditional oath stating that as long as they were not forced to take up arms against France, they would remain loyal to the British. Although there is some debate among historians, Gov. Richard Phillips is said to have accepted the Acadians' conditional allegiance in 1730, but simply forgot or failed to inform authorities.

CRIME TIME

In the latest available data, it takes an average of:

- 336 days to resolve murder cases
- 209 days to resolve sexual assault cases
- 263 days to resolve drug trafficking cases
- 24 percent of cases were stayed, withdrawn, dismissed or discharged.
- Of all Canadian provinces, Nova Scotia has the lowest incarceration rate; 23 percent of all guilty charges applied in the province result in incarceration.
- One in eight Nova Scotians charged with a crime ends up in jail.

In 1755, in response to French authorities building Fort Beauséjour on the present-day Nova Scotia/New Brunswick border, the English again raised this issue of the refusal by Acadians to swear their unconditional loyalty to England. This time, however, England began what is the most traumatic chapter in Acadian history. They claimed the entire Acadian population as prisoners, and from Beauséjour to Grand Pré, they loaded the Acadians onto boats destined for the colonies to the south.

From 1755 to 1762, it is estimated that three-quarters of the 13,000-strong Acadian population was deported; others fled, establishing remote Acadian communities that existed quietly on the fringes of society. Those who were deported were not only stripped of the land that they had spent a century or more cultivating, but they were only allowed to take the most basic of their possessions with them. In their wake, their villages were burned to the ground.

When Henry Wadsworth Longfellow's epic poem Evangeline was published in the United States in 1847, the story of the deportation and Le Grand Dérangement ("The Great Uprooting") was told to the English-speaking world. It was an immediate sensation and now has been translated into more than 130 languages. What Evangeline did was rescue the Acadians from being just a footnote in the history of the New World, to being a resilient people, with a proud and enduring culture of their own.

- The average median sentence of jail time in Nova Scotia is 55 days.
- 37 percent of Nova Scotian sentences are for less than a month.
- Only six percent of those sentenced spend more than a year in prison.

THE COST OF CRIME
Crime takes a toll on Nova Scotian wallets.
- In the latest available data, crime costs Nova Scotians $297 per household. Nationally, crime costs Canadian households $319.
- In total, crime costs Nova Scotians $102.42 million a year.
- Break and entries cost Nova Scotians $21.8 million.
- Vehicle theft: $9.5 million
- Robbery: $1.25 million
- Theft: $47.2 million
- Fraud: $14.3 million
- Vandalism: $8.4 million

TOLL ON HEALTH
Nova Scotians spent 2,412 days in hospital recovering as the victims of crimes, in the latest data from Statistics Canada.
- Each day of care cost $662 per patient, per day.

Take 5 — TOP FIVE COMMUNITIES WITH THE MOST POLICE (PER CAPITA)

1. **Annapolis Royal**
2. **Kentville**
3. **Bridgewater**
4. **Amherst**
5. **Trenton**

IMPACT ON SOCIETY

Corrections as a whole cost Nova Scotians more than $75 million a year.

- It costs more than $120 million to police the province .
- It costs Nova Scotian taxpayers $121/day or $44,165/year for each incarcerated person in the province.
- It costs $1,344 per year to pay for a prisoner's probation.

SURVEY SEZ . . . THERE GOES THE NEIGHBOURHOOD

- Percentage of Nova Scotians who feel very safe walking alone after dark in their neighbourhoods: 44
- Percentage who feel reasonably safe: 37
- Percentage who feel very unsafe: 6

The First People

The Mi'kmaq are Nova Scotia's First People. Mi'kmaw territory, known as Mi'kma'ki, included mainland Nova Scotia and Cape Breton as well as New Brunswick, Prince Edward Island, the Gaspé Peninsula and Newfoundland. Traditionally, Mi'kmaw territory was divided into seven districts, each with its own distinct meaning:

Wunama'kik: "foggy land" – Cape Breton Island

Piwktuk: "where gaseous explosions erupt" – Pictou and P.E.I.

Eskikewa'kik : "skin dressers' territory" – Guysborough and Halifax counties

Sipekne'katik : "ground nut place" – Halifax, Lunenburg, Kings, Hants and Colchester Counties

Kespukwitk: "lands end" – Queens, Shelburne, Yarmouth, Digby and Annapolis Counties

Siknikt: "drainage place" – Cumberland County and the New Brunswick counties of Westmoreland, Albert, Kent, St. John, Kings and Queens

Kespek: "last land" – north of the Richibucto River and parts of Gaspé

- In 1860 the Mi'kmaq added an eighth district, **Taqamkuk**, southern Newfoundland.

- The word Mi'kmaq means "my friends." The Mi'kmaq originally identified themselves as L'nu'k, "the people." The word Mi'kmaw is the adjective form of Mi'kmaq.

LANGUAGE

The Mi'kmaw language, known by speakers as Mi'kmawi'simk, is a dialect of the Algonquian language stock, one of the two main Northeastern languages (the other is Iroquoian). It is related to other Native American languages like Ojibwe and Cree. Today the Mi'kmaw language has a written alphabet, but was traditionally conveyed orally or through pictographs. Contrary to popular belief, Mi'kmaw pictographs are not derived from Ancient Egyptian or Mayan hieroglyphs; they are North American in origin.

MI'KMAW PLACE NAMES AND THEIR MEANINGS

Antigonish: "where branches are torn off" – perhaps a reference to a location where bears would come to eat beechnuts or hazelnuts
Chezzetcook: "flowing rapidly in many channels"
Eskasoni: "green boughs"
Joggins: "a place of fish weirs"
Kejimkujik (Lake): "attempting to escape," or it may also mean "swelled private parts," a reference to the physical toll of an eight km paddle across the lake

Did you know...

That there are several different Mi'kmaw dialects? Though all Mi'kmaq speakers can easily understand one another, the language spoken by Mi'kmaq in Cape Breton differs from that of New Brunswick.

(Lake) Banook: "first lake in a chain"

Malagash: "place of games"

Merigomish: "a place of merry-making"

Musquodoboit: "suddenly widening out after a narrow entrance
at its mouth"

Pictou: "an explosion"

Shubenacadie: "place where ground nuts occur"

Tancook (Island): "out to sea"

Tidnish: "paddle"

Tusket: "a great forked tidal river"

SUBSISTENCE

Before and after the arrival of Europeans, the Mi'kmaq used their land
in a pattern of seasonal migrations and settlements. In the winter they
moved inland where they lived in small family-based villages and
hunted large game, such as moose and bear. For the bulk of the year,
the Mi'kmaq relocated to larger villages at estuaries and on the coast
where they relied more heavily upon the sea for sustenance. Although
Mi'kmaq depended primarily on game, fish and foraged food (such as
berries and wild plants), it is also possible that they grew crops.

HOUSING

Traditionally, the Mi'kmaq lived in "wigwams," a word derived from
the Mi'kmaw term wikuom. Women were responsible for building
these conical watertight dwellings of birchbark, and could erect one in
a single day. At their largest, wigwams could house 12 to 15 people.

Did you know...

That the word "toboggan" comes from the Mi'kmaw word taba'gan.

HOW TO BUILD A WIGWAM

The frame of a wigwam consists of five spruce poles tied together at the top with split spruce root and spread out at the bottom to make a cone shape. Tie a hoop of moosewood around the poles, just down from the top, to brace them. Then tie shorter poles to the hoop to provide sup-

Take 5 DANIEL PAUL'S
FIVE IMPORTANT NOVA SCOTIA MI'KMAQ

Born on the Indian Brook Reserve near Shubenacadie, Daniel Paul is a passionate Mi'kmaw historian, writer, and social commentator. In detailing a past that standard history books have chosen to ignore, he seeks to teach people of the damage that racism can do. His book, *We Were Not the Savages*, is a disturbing account of the genocidal tactics – including scalp bounties, starvation and germ warfare – used by British colonial officials in an attempt to extermi-nate and subjugate the Mi'kmaq. Paul was the founding executive director of the Confederacy of Mainland Micmacs, and is a member of the Order of Nova Scotia. When asked for his list of five most important Mi'kmaw leaders, he replied, "I have too much respect for the hundreds of individuals from our community who have made a difference for the Mi'kmaq to name five as my favourites. Therefore, I'll do five at random of the hundreds of my favourites."

1. **Chief Jean Baptiste Cope (Kopit)** (1698-176?), Shubenacadie Mi'kmaq District. With the Treaty of 1752 and entering into a Friendship treaty with British Governor Peregrine Thomas Hopson, Chief Kopit laid the foundation for the modern day recog-nition of Mi'kmaw treaty rights by the Supreme Court of Canada.

2. **Former Pictou Landing Chief Raymond Francis**. Chief Francis, by determinedly opposing the use of Boat Harbour as an industrial waste lagoon, and resolutely seeking redress for the grievous

port for the cover of birchbark. Lay birchbark sheets over the poles like shingles, starting from the bottom and overlapping them. Extra poles can be laid over the outside to hold the sheets of birchbark down. Keep the top left of the roof open to allow smoke from a fireplace to escape. In bad weather a detachable piece of birchbark can cover this "chim-

wrong done to the band, single-handedly kept pushing until the Band acquired legal counsel and sued its trustee. An out-of-court settlement is nearing $50 million, and a cleanup is in the works.

3. **Former Membertou Chief Ben Christmas** (1896-1966). In the late 1930s and early 1940s, senior Department of Indian Affairs bureaucrats decided that they would centralize the Mi'kmaq of Nova Scotia into two reserves. Chief Ben Christmas stands tall among those who fought diligently to end their disgraceful attempt to ethnically cleanse the Mi'kmaq

4. **Sister Dorothy Moore**, Mi'kmaw teacher. Sister Moore is largely responsible for many of the positive inclusions of Mi'kmaw history and culture in Nova Scotia's school curriculum. She is a strong supporter of human rights for all peoples, and has fought diligently for equal opportunities for all.

5. **Elsie Basque**, first licensed Mi'kmaq teacher in Nova Scotia. Licensed in 1937, Elsie Basque successfully applied by mail to the Inverness County School Inspector for a teaching job at Mabou Ridge. When he met her, he advised that it would be best for her to go home because he felt that Mabou Ridge people would never accept a Mi'kmaq to teach their children. She refused to be intimidated and stayed.

ney." Line floors with fir twigs, woven mats and animal furs. A large hide (such as that of a moose) can be used as a door cover.

BIRCHBARK CANOE

This ingenious vessel allowed the Mi'kmaq to travel the tempestuous east coast of Mi'kma'ki, sometimes as far as Newfoundland. The first task in building an 18 to 24-foot canoe was to find a large birch tree that could provide the necessary bark. The frame or 'ribs' of the canoe was made of cedar slats. The ribs were then covered in sheets of birchbark sewn together with fir roots. Birchbark canoes were waterproofed using fir gum chewed by women and children. Canoes of the ocean-going Mi'kmaq had elevated gunwales to prevent waves from splashing into the craft and were propelled using beech paddles. After Europeans arrived, sails were also used.

SNOWSHOES

An innovative Mi'kmaw technology, snowshoes allowed the people to hunt and travel in Nova Scotia's deep winter snow. Men shaped strips of wood into oval waist-high frames, with curved ends tied together with moose leather. Centre supports were made using two slats of wood across the frame, about two hands apart. Women then took over the process and corded the frames in a crisscross fashion to support the toe, foot and heel.

MARRIAGE

Polygamy, though uncommon, was practiced by the Mi'kmaq. More commonly, however, marriage was a life-long union between couples.

Did you know...

That the word tipi was never used by the Mi'kmaq? It was a term used by another aboriginal group and refers to a dwelling made of skins, not birchbark.

Before a wedding, the hopeful groom gave gifts to the bride's father to demonstrate his worthiness. If the union was approved, the couple was married in a days-long celebration that featured a feast provided by the groom, as well as games, singing and dancing. Weddings also provided an opportunity for the Mi'kmaq to recite their family trees – not uncommonly stretching back as far as ten generations! Although marriage was highly esteemed, the union could be ended by either spouse.

DIVISION OF LABOUR

Mi'kmaw men and women had different responsibilities based on gender, which were taught to children at a young age. Men hunted, made equipment (such bows, arrows, lances, snowshoe frames and canoes), and when it was required, engaged in warfare and diplomacy. Women were responsible for preparing food, gathering water and food, fishing and gathering shellfish and berries, tending children, transporting and skinning game, preparing hides and making clothing, crafting birch-bark dishes, boxes and baskets, weaving mats, setting up wigwams, and transporting camp equipment.

GAMES

Games had an important place in Mi'kmaq society, as they cemented relationships between communities. The Mi'kmaq gambled, played a dice game, and enjoyed ball games using a ball made of caribou hide and stuffed with caribou fur. They also competed in bow-and-arrow contests and engaged in foot, canoe and swimming races.

MI'KMAW SPIRITUALITY

The Mi'kmaq believed the invisible, omnipresent and omnipotent Creator, the Great Spirit, created the universe. Like many aboriginal groups, they were animistic, seeing humans as part of a multilayered universe in which all animals and objects contain an identity and spiritual essence. All animals and things have 'person' features, and people, animals and objects can change shape. The spiritual world and the physical

133

environment are not separate, and they interact continuously. For example, the Mi'kmaq believed animals could reincarnate themselves from small segments of their bodies. This belief is what underlies the Mi'kmaw teaching that all parts of a killed animal must be respected and preserved.

A puoin is a highly respected person who communicates with the unseen spirit world. Aided by a medicine bag containing bones, pebbles, carvings and other sacred objects, puoins had important powers. They could locate game and fish, forecast the weather and predict the actions of spirit-beings.

MYTHS

Myths and stories serve a very important purpose in Mi'kmaw culture. They are intended to teach children how things came to be and to explain the workings of the universe. They serve as a constant reminder to the people of their place in the complex universe.

KLUSCAP (GLOOSCAP)

One of the most important figures in Mi'kmaw mythology is Kluscap. Given his power by the Great Spirit, Kluscap was regarded as an important creator and teacher of the Mi'kmaw people. He created Mi'kma'ki and all its animals, giving them their shape and size. He also taught the Mi'kmaq to hunt, fish, cultivate and travel by the stars.

Kluscap lived in a wigwam at Cape Blomidon, which he shared with his family, an adopted grandmother and a young boy named Marten. From there, his hunting ground was far ranging and included Newfoundland, the Maritimes, Maine and Quebec's Gaspé Peninsula. When Kluscap's work was done — when he had finished creating and teaching the Mi'kmaq people — he hosted a great feast for the Mi'kmaq at Blomidon. Then he left the people, stepping into his canoe made of stone, and paddled out to sea. As he left he told them that those who lived kind and just lives would live forever beside him. No one knows where he went, but he travelled up a peaceful river where he waits until the day he returns to the people.

Another home of Kluscap is Kelly's Mountain in Cape Breton, which is regarded as a sacred site in Mi'kmaw cosmology.

PETROGLYPHS

Petroglyphs are drawings etched in rock that are found around mainland Nova Scotia. They depict hunting and fishing scenes, Mi'kmaw myths and rituals, and supernatural figures. There are about 50,000 of these rock drawings at Kejimkujik National Park. Sites have also been found on the Bedford Barrens and outside of Dartmouth. A prominent theme in Mi'kmaw rock art is the culloo, a long-necked, heron-like bird. Records from the 17th century show that the culloo was seen by the Mi'kmaq as playing an important role in transporting the soul to the other world.

THE SOUL

The Mi'kmaq believed humans were made of three elements: the body, the 'life soul' (the activity of the heart, lungs, circulation and motor functions) and the 'free soul,' which existed outside the physical form and was a shadow of the person. There were two varieties of free souls: those of the living and those of the dead. After death, the free soul travelled to the 'Land of the Souls,' but could return to earth to haunt the living. The Mi'kmaw afterlife was peaceful for all.

MI'KMAW FUNERALS

Death was not a prerequisite for a Mi'kmaw funeral. In some cases, a funeral would be held for the incurably ill, before they died. The dying individual would offer a farewell speech, which was followed by feasting and dancing. Tobacco was important in funeral rites, as offering tobacco to the spirits aided the dead in getting to the spirit world. Dogs were often killed as a sign of grief and spouses mourned their dead husband or wife for a year. Every ten years or so, the Mi'kmaw dead were brought together and buried at a single site – an event that was also celebrated with feasts, dancing and speeches.

MI'KMAW CATHOLICISM

The Mi'kmaq were first exposed to Roman Catholicism when the French settled in Mi'kma'ki in the early 17th century. Their attitude towards this new religion was one of both curiosity and openness. They allowed Jesuit priests to live and work among them, and in 1610, Grand Chief Membertou became the first Mi'kmaq to convert to Christianity. Remarkably, the Mi'kmaq accepted the spirituality of the Catholic Church without abandoning their own religious views; they saw Jesus as a natural brother to Klooscap.

The special relationship with the Catholic Church was formalized in a 1610 agreement between the Mi'kmaq and the Vatican known as the Mi'kmaq Concordat. With this treaty, which was spelled out on a wampum belt, the Mi'kmaq agreed to protect French settlers and priests in their territory and gave the Catholic Church access to Mi'kmaw lands for the purpose of building churches. In return, the Church recognized the Mi'kmaq as a Nation with its own inherent laws, customs, and religious authority.

This blending of the two traditions into one distinct faith remains strong today as Mi'kmaq Catholicism. The patron saint of the Mi'kmaq is St Anne, the grandmother of Jesus Christ. On July 26th the Mi'kmaq celebrate 'the Grandmother' in St Anne's Day celebrations across the province, and especially at Chapel Island, Cape Breton.

MI'KMAW HEALING

The Mi'kmaq had the power to heal using their ingenuity, spiritual guidance, and knowledge of natural resources. They used emetics to induce vomiting, while swellings or boils were treated with blood-letting incisions. A favourite remedy for an open wound was the application of a piece of beaver kidney, which served to absorb blood and pus. The Mi'kmaw treatment for drowning was one that both alarmed and impressed early Europeans. The apparently lifeless victim would be administered a smoke enema, and then was hanged from a tree by the ankles until he revived. Early Europeans benefited much from

Mi'kmaw medicine – the Mi'kmaw cure for scurvy, a tea made of alder, saved the lives of explorer Jacques Cartier and his crew in 1534.

SWEAT LODGE

Sweat lodges are important to Mi'kmaq spiritual and physical health. These lodges, a wigwam frame covered in birchbark and skins, featured a shallow pit that holds red-hot stones that have been heated in a fire. For an hour at a time, Mi'kmaq men sit naked around the pit, chanting, meditating and telling legends. At the end of this ritual, the men would run to a nearby lake or roll in the snow.

MI'KMAW HERBAL MEDICINES

(Don't try this at home! If used incorrectly it may be poisonous.)

The Mi'kmaq used a number of poultices and drinks to prevent illness and to heal and cure disease:

Ground Juniper: Ailment: kidney ailments, especially bladder infections, diabetes. **Application:** Juniper twigs are cut off at the ends and boiled to make a drinkable tonic.

White Spruce Tree: Ailment: colds, tuberculosis, laryngitis, mouth sores. **Application:** for lung ailments, a cup of tonic made of boiled branches and bark should be consumed at least twice a day. Sap can be scraped from the bark and applied to mouth sores.

Alder: Ailment: rheumatism, stomach and kidney problems, fever, neuralgia and migraine headaches. **Application:** Soak shavings from the inner bark in water, along with a dash of peppermint. The shavings are then applied to the person's head, and held in place by a towel-wrap. The towel and the shavings should be replaced daily.

Cherry Tree: Ailment: colds, flu **Application:** boil the bark for an hour, then drink two cups of the tonic a day.

Flagroot: Ailment: preventatively, for colds, coughs, flu, stomach ailments and colic in babies. **Application:** ingest the root of the plant. When combined with sarsaparilla makes a cough medicine.

Golden Thread: Ailment: stomach ulcers, diarrhea, colds, influenza, diabetes, chapped lips, cuts and abrasions. **Application:** steep as a tea. For external use, can be boiled with animal fat and once cooled, used as a salve.

POLITICAL STRUCTURE
There were three levels of leadership in Mi'kma'ki: local, district and regional. Each Mi'kmaw community was headed by a sagamore, or chief. Sagamores were selected according to a number of criteria: To a degree, leadership was hereditary, often being passed down the male lineage from father to son or nephew. But a leader also had to demonstrate his ability as a hunter or a warrior, and sagamores who did a poor job were not tolerated.

Sagamores did not rule dictatorially, but by persuasion. Generosity was highly valued in chiefs; as the best and cleverest hunter, a sagamore would provide food and furs for his people, and receive nothing in return. District and regional chiefs participated in the Mi'kmaq Grand Council.

THE GRAND COUNCIL
The Grand Council (Sante' Mawiomi) was the governing body that united Mi'kma'ki. It consisted of sagamores elected from each of the seven territorial districts, who in turn elected a kji'saqmaw, or Grand Chief, the ceremonial head of state. The other officers of the Grand Council were the Grand Captain (kji'keptan), who advised on political affairs, and a putus, who remembered the treaties and kept the constitution.

Several times a year, the Grand Council met to decide where families might hunt, fish and set up camp. They also dealt with relations with other First Nations. When the Mi'kmaq embraced Catholicism in the 17th century, St Anne's Day became an important meeting time of the Grand Council. Today, Grand Council representatives are community chiefs.

THE WABANAKI CONFEDERACY

The Mi'kmaq were also part of a larger political organization, the Wabanaki Confederacy. This was a loose coalition of five eastern Algonquian tribes who banded together to counter Iroquois aggression and collaborate on the bigger issues of diplomacy, war and trade. The other nations were the Maliseet, Passamaquoddy, Penobscot, and the Abenaki of present-day New Brunswick, Maine, New Hampshire and Vermont. Although the confederacy officially disbanded in 1862, the five tribes remain close allies today.

TREATIES

During the 18th century, as France and Britain vied for control of North America, the Mi'kmaq were important players in the conflict. No mere pawns in the imperial struggle, the Mi'kmaq sided with France and actively fought to drive the British out of their lands. Beginning in 1725, Mi'kmaq-British animosity began to subside when a "treaty of peace and friendship" was signed between the two nations. Subsequent treaties followed in 1728, 1749, 1752 and 1760. The Mi'kmaq agreed to "bury the hatchet" and cease their attacks on the British. Although they did not surrender their sovereignty or land ownership, the Mi'kmaq agreed to allow the British to use their lands. In return, the British promised to protect Mi'kmaq territory and to allow the Mi'kmaq to continue hunting and fishing "unmolested."

In 1999, the Supreme Court's Marshall decision was a landmark recognition of these earlier treaty rights. It determined that the treaties signed between the Mi'kmaq and the British in 1760 give the Mi'kmaq a communal right to hunt, fish and gather in pursuit of a "moderate livelihood." A later court ruling would place limits on this right.

Did you know...

That October 1st is Treaty Day, an annual day to remember Anglo-Mi'kmaq treaties and their ongoing importance.

CENTRALIZATION

By the early 1900's, the Mi'kmaq were living on 40 small reserves scattered around Nova Scotia. Beginning in 1942, the Government of Canada embarked on a policy of centralization that saw the relocation of over 2,000 Nova Scotia Mi'kmaq onto two main reserves: Eskasoni in Cape Breton, and Shubenacadie, on the mainland. Each of these reserves doubled in size as a result.

The government believed that this relocation would improve its ability to efficiently provide services to the Mi'kmaq. The plan, however, was disastrous for the natives. They were not consulted about the move, and many felt coerced to relocate, threatened with the prospect of losing federal services.

Many had given up good farm land to move to new locations that had poor soil. What the two communities also lacked was adequate housing and employment opportunities. The centralization policy was essentially abandoned by 1949. When the promised benefits of the new communities failed to materialize, many Mi'kmaq undertook the arduous task of re-establishing themselves in their former communities.

THE MI'KMAQ TODAY

Today 12,261 registered indigenous people, most of them Mi'kmaq, live in Nova Scotia. Most live on 13 reserves, eight of which are on the mainland and five on Cape Breton Island. Approximately 4,000

They Said It

"The stated purpose of this exercise [centralization] was to make it easier for bureaucrats to administer our people at two central locations. But the effect was to take more of our people off the land, deny them their livelihood and force them to live on two overcrowded containment centers."

– Alex Christmas, President of the Union of Nova Scotia Indians, Eskasoni, 1992

Mi'kmaq live off-reserve.

About one in three Mi'kmaq speaks the Mi'kmaq language. In recent years, there has been a growing interest in preserving and revitalizing the language. In 1997, Mi'kmaq Online, a talking online dictionary, was launched featuring seven words and two sentences; today the site boasts more than 6,000 words as well as stories and songs.

In 1992, history was made when Eleanor Johnson of Eskasoni wrote the first Masters thesis entirely in the Mi'kmaq language. Johnson's Mi'kmaq was written for the Anthropology Department at Saint Mary's University in Halifax.

POET LAUREATE: RITA JOE

Rita Joe was born at Whycocomagh, Cape Breton in 1932 to Josie and Annie Bernard. As a young woman she met and married Frank Joe, and the couple moved to Eskasoni where they raised ten children. In 1973, Joe began her illustrious career as an author, writing stories and poems for the *Micmac News*.

By 1978, she had collected her poems into her first published collection, *Poems of Rita Joe*. Several more poetry and story collections, as well as an autobiography, followed. These solidified Joe's position as one of Canada's most accomplished writers. Her critically and popularly acclaimed writings have also earned her the unofficial title of poet laureate of the Mi'kmaw people. Her writing captures the beauty and complexity of Mi'kmaw culture – but more than that, it challenges the negative images that often stereotype aboriginal people.

Rita Joe explains her mission as a writer: "I want to put out positive images of aboriginal people. But everything I do is gentle persuasion. And that had more effect than a blockade or any other way – kindness, always. I teach my people to do the same."

Rita Joe and her work have been honoured with many awards. She has won the Nova Scotia Writers Federation Prize, received several honorary degrees, and in 1990, she was made a member of the Order of Canada.

Not Black and White

Tolerance means nothing if it doesn't mean the acceptance of difference and therefore the preservation and maintenance of difference.
  – George Elliott Clarke

THE SLAVERY FACT
Until 1833, Nova Scotia, like much of North America, was a slave-owning society. Many of the first black settlers in Nova Scotia were slaves and the relationship between black and white Nova Scotians was determined by this fact. Black people were widely held to be second-class citizens, and as non-citizens when they were the property of whites.

SLAVES AT LOUISBOURG
Between 1713 and 1758, at least 266 slaves lived on Cape Breton Island (then known as Ile Royale). Most lived at Louisbourg where they were domestic servants in French households.

THE "PECULIAR INSTITUTION" IN EARLY HALIFAX
The French did not have a monopoly on slave holding. Early English Halifax also accepted slavery as part of life. In 1751, a schooner named *Success* landed at Halifax, bringing "nine negro men" from Antigua. In 1752, a Halifax merchant offered to sell one female and five male

slaves. The woman was described as ". . . a very likely Negro Wench, of about thirty five years of Age . . . and (was) capable of doing all sorts of Work belonging thereto, as Needlework of all sorts and in the best manner, also Washing, Ironing, Cookery and every other thing that can be expected from such a slave."

Twenty Dollars Reward

Halifax Weekly Chronicle, 15 March 1794:
Twenty Dollars Reward

Ran away, on Thursday evening, the 18th inst a Negro Man Servant, the property of the Subscriber, named BELFAST; but who commonly goes by the name of BILL . . . At the time of the elopement he was in the service of William Forsyth, Esq.; and had meditated an attempt to get on board a ship that night which lay in the harbour, bound to Newfoundland; but was frustrated: It is probable, however, he may still endeavour to escape that way, therefore, the masters of all coasters going along shore, or other vessels bound to sea, are hereby forewarned from carrying him off at their peril, as they will be prosecuted, if discovered, with the utmost rigour of the law.

The above reward will be paid to any person or persons who shall apprehend and secure him, so that I may recover him again.

He is a likely, stout-made fellow, of five feet eight or nine inches high, and about 27 years of age; of a mild good countenance and features, smooth black skin, with very white teeth; is a native of South Carolina, speaks good English, and very softly, and has been in this Province ten years.

When he went off, he wore an old Bath-Coating short coat, of a light colour, wore out at the elbows; brown cloth or duffil trowsers, also much wore at the knees; a round hat, and an old black silk handkerchief about his neck:— But as he had other cloaths secreted in town, he may have changed his whole apparel.

He will no doubt endeavour to pass for a free man, and possibly by some other name. – **MICHAEL WALLACE**

SLAVE OWNERS

On July 29, 1779, a Planter, Matthew Arnold, recorded that he sold "one Negro boy named Abraham now about 12 years of age, who was born of my Negro slave in my house in Maryland, for and in consideration of fifty pounds currency." For all their idealism about freedom, slavery still had a place in the Planter world.

BLACK LOYALISTS

One of the first groups of blacks to settle Nova Scotia were from the 13 American Colonies and loyal to the Crown during the American Revolution.

- 3,500 blacks living in the 13 Colonies came to Nova Scotia to join the 500 blacks, both slave and free, who already called the colony home.
- Black Loyalists were enticed by loyalty as well as promises of land and freedom.
- Black Loyalists found Nova Scotia's promises of land and of equal rights to be hollow. Each family head had been promised 100 acres of free land, plus fifty acres for each person in the house hold. Black military officers were to receive 1000 acres and privates, 100 acres. Such allotments never materialized.
- Only one third of black Loyalists received any land at all.
- On average, black Loyalists received fewer than 12 acres of land.
- Lands granted to black Loyalists were the infertile, often rocky tracts unwanted by white Loyalists.
- Black Loyalists found themselves competing with whites for work, and thanks to prejudice, often lost out in this competition.

Did you know...

That it was only in 1833 that the British Parliament passed the Imperial Act, which abolished slavery in the whole British Empire, including Nova Scotia.

RACIAL TENSIONS IN SHELBURNE

More than 1,500 black Loyalists settled at Shelburne, Nova Scotia, a town that was, in the late 18th century, experiencing unemployment and underemployment. Tense race relations existed in Shelburne from the outset. White Loyalists sought to drive black Loyalists out of town, mainly because black Loyalists worked for lower wages, undercutting white employment opportunities.

Tensions reached fever pitch when a black Baptist minister, David George, began to baptize whites. Although authorities did not disallow George's sacraments, George became the target of racially motivated attacks. A mob of hundreds of whites gathered, tearing down George's home, as well as those of his followers. Black residents of Shelburne were beaten and driven from town.

Fleeing black Loyalists re-established themselves at nearby

Bio   MARY POSTELL

Mary Postell, a slave and daughter of a rebel officer, sought refuge with the British during the American Revolution and was granted her Certificate of Freedom. The document, however, would later be stolen and Postell would pay an enormous price.

After the war, and unable to prove her freedom, Postell moved to Florida where she found she was sold and resold by several 'owners.' When her master, Jesse Gray, moved to Nova Scotia, he took Postell with him. Fearing she would be sold again, Postell and her two children escaped Gray. She was found in Birchtown, however, and went on trial for her freedom.

At Postell's trial, two free blacks from Birchtown testified as witnesses on her behalf. For doing this, their homes were torched, and one of their children killed. Although Jesse Gray had misplaced his bill of sale for Postell, the courts sided with him and she was returned to him as his rightful 'property.' To punish his errant slave, Gray sold Postell for 100 bushels of potatoes.

Birchtown, leaving behind their homes and belongings. No aid was offered to the relocated blacks.

NOVA SCOTIA BORN

The percentage of the Halifax population that is African Canadians is four percent, the third highest proportion of any city in the country, behind Toronto and Montreal, according to the latest census.

- Chance that an African Canadian living in Halifax is third generation Nova Scotian or beyond, according to Canadian Social Trends: 8 in 10

- Chance that an African Canadian living elsewhere in Canada's cities is a third generation Canadian or beyond: 1 in 10

SEARCH FOR THE PROMISED LAND CONTINUES: SIERRA LEONE

Black Loyalists did not find their hopes realized in Nova Scotia. Discrimination and poverty became their lot. A number of black Loyalists considered other options. Led by David George, a group of Loyalists accepted an invitation made by the Sierra Leone Company, a philanthropic organization that invited Nova Scotia blacks to relocate to the African Country of Sierra Leone. In January 1792, 15 ships containing 1,200 black Loyalists - about a third of all the blacks living in Nova Scotia - sailed to Sierra Leone.

MAROONS

Another group of black Nova Scotians, the Maroons, originated in the British colony of Jamaica. For 140 years, beginning in 1655, Maroons fought their British colonizers. In 1796, they were subdued by the Jamaican government and the British deported the independent-minded Maroons. Five hundred and forty-three Maroon men, women and children were shipped to Halifax, where they landed in July 1796.

Like the black Loyalists, the Maroons had high hopes for the freedoms they would enjoy in Nova Scotia; like the Loyalists, they were quickly disillusioned. After two hard winters, many Maroons followed black Loyalists to Sierra Leone.

REFUGEES OF WAR

A third wave of black settlement in Nova Scotia coincided with the War of 1812. During the conflict, blacks in the United States sought the protection of the British. Two to three thousand refugees were brought by ship to Halifax in 1815. Most of these settled around Preston and Hammonds Plains.

THE BAPTIST CONNECTION

Early black settlers in Nova Scotia found themselves excluded from the official Anglican churches of the colony. As a result, distinct black religious traditions emerged. Some of the earliest black settlers in Nova Scotia were well-respected clergy and would later be ordained by the Baptist church. While some, such as Shelburne's David George,

Did you know...

That people living in the communities of Preston, Upper Hammonds Plains, Guysborough, Lincolnville, Tracadie, Milford Haven and Boylston can trace their roots to the escaped slaves of the 19th century Underground Railroad. Traveling by night, relying on the constellations for direction, the runaways made their way from the American South through waterways, swamps, forests, mountains and back roads to the free northern states and to Canada.

With the assistance of such groups as the Quakers, free blacks and Native Americans, these bonded men, women and children were able to gain their freedom. At least 20,000 slaves escaped to Canada via the Underground Railroad, most of them crossing the border in Southern Ontario. Some of these refugees then made their way to Nova Scotia.

ministered to black and white alike, perhaps the greatest legacy of Baptist clergy was the community and fellowship their congregations inspired. Baptist churches became important sites of cultural, social and political activities in black communities.

WE DID IT FIRST: FIRST AFRICAN BAPTIST CHURCH

In 1832, the Cornwallis Street Baptist Church, the first African Baptist church in Nova Scotia was founded in Halifax by Rev. Richard Preston.

WE DID IT FIRST: FIRST WORLD BOXING
TITLE TO A BLACK MAN

In 1890, Halifax-born George Dixon won the World Bantam weight boxing title, becoming the first black ever to win a boxing title.

AFRICVILLE

The story of the Africville relocation is one of the most heart breaking in Canadian history. Africville, also known as Seaview, was a thriving black community on the outskirts of Halifax, on the Bedford Basin. It was settled by former slaves after the War of 1812.

Over time, the community grew to be a slum, in part a result of neglect heaped upon it by the City of Halifax. Africville was denied such basic city services as paved roads, street lights, running water, sewage

Take 5 TOP FIVE FAMOUS BLACK NOVA SCOTIANS

1. **Portia White**, actress and singer
2. **William Hall**, "Victoria cross recipient"
3. **George Elliott Clarke**, poet and novelist
4. **Dr. Marie Hamilton**, first African Canadian woman to receive Governor General's award
5. **Wayne Smith**, CFL player

and electricity. As the city expanded, Africville became the preferred site for such undesirable operations and facilities as a prison, a slaughterhouse, and a sewage dumping station. Although Africville was seen as a community of the destitute and downtrodden, the social cohesion amongst its residents was strong.

In the 1960s, Halifax City Council began to consider relocating residents, an option made all the more attractive by the vast business potential of the site. Proposed urban development plans included the construction of the A. Murray McKay Bridge and its related highway interchange system, and the Port of Halifax development at Fairview Cove. In 1967, the city evicted the residents of Africville. Without deeds to prove their ownership of the land on which they had lived for 150 years, residents could not fight the city's plans. Paid $500 for their troubles, families were forced to leave their community and settle in poorly constructed public housing developments in Uniacke Square, Mulgrave Park and Spryfield.

DATES TO REMEMBER

- 1945: the Nova Scotia Association for the Advancement of Coloured People (NSAACP), a social reform organization, was founded.
- 1954: Nova Scotia desegregation laws passed.
- 1969: Black United Front established. For 12 years the organization fought discrimination in Nova Scotia, until it disbanded in 1981.
- 1993: Wayne Adams elected to the provincial legislature, its first black member.
- 2001 George Elliott Clarke wins the Governor General's Literary Award for poetry.

Did you know...

That in 2002, Africville was named a National Historic Site. Unveiling the site marker, Heritage Minister Sheila Copps said of the Africville debacle, "As the fabric has been torn apart, so the fabric can be mended. And what we're doing today is the beginning of a process that I hope will place the name of Africville on the lips of every Canadian."

WE DID IT FIRST: FIRST BLACK WOMAN MAYOR IN CANADA

In 1984, Daurene Lewis was elected Mayor of the town of Annapolis Royal, the first time in Canadian history that a black woman is elected town mayor.

CORRECTING HISTORY

In 2004, Nova Scotia's Black History week celebrated its twentieth birthday. The first such celebration was held in 1984, hosted by the Halifax North Memorial Public Library. In 1989, it became a month-long celebration.

THE IMPORTANCE OF PLACE: AFRICADIA

George Elliott Clarke coined the term Africadia to designate the land, history, and even the past and present existence of black Nova Scotians. Explaining this term, Clarke says, "I'm interested in re-writing the map of Nova Scotia. ...In the same way that the Mi'kmaq people have gone back to original Mi'kmaq names for many of the places in this province in order to lay claim to it, we need to reclaim the province because we have been disenfranchised; we've been ignored, we've been erased, in a sense, from the map."

KIRK JOHNSON: A BOXER FIGHTS THE SYSTEM

In April 1998, heavyweight boxer Kirk Johnson of North Preston was pulled over by five police cars, and his vehicle seized by an officer who claimed he did not have the correct papers for his car (he did). The next day, his car was returned, without apology.

Arguing that he had been the victim of racism and targeted as a result of racial profiling, Johnson brought his case before a Nova Scotia Human

Did you know...

That the United Nations has called on the Nova Scotia government to compensate the families displaced by the Africville relocation.

Rights tribunal. The boxer accused the Halifax police officers of pulling him over for "driving while black." The tribunal ruled that Johnson had indeed been a victim of racism. While the Chief of Police issued an apology, the head of the Police Association continued to deny that racism had been a factor. Johnson was awarded $10,000 in penalties.

"IT'S TIME TO RECLAIM THE SCHOOL"

These words were spoken by Halifax Regional School superintendent Don Trider in the aftermath of an October 2, 1997 conflict between black and white students at Cole Harbour High School. On October 1st, a black and a white student engaged in a lunch hour fistfight. Later that afternoon, 40 students refused to attend class and hurled epithets at school staff. More than a dozen students were suspended.

The next day, the discord continued. When a fire alarm was pulled and the school evacuated, fights erupted in the schoolyard. As teach-

They Said It

"The area is not suited for residences but properly developed is ideal for industrial purposes. There is water frontage for piers, the railway for sidings, a road to be developed leading directly downtown and in the other direction to the provincial highway."
– 1954 report by Halifax City Manager, explaining a reason for the relocation

"It's true I have a nicer home and I have hot and cold water and a bathroom but I haven't got happiness, that's one thing I haven't got . . . if Africville was built up again, I'd be the first to move back, I would."
– Former Africville resident

"There was just that sense of anywhere you go, anywhere you fall down, you hurt yourself, you don't have to go home, you go to the nearest house, then have that taken care of."
– Terry Dixon, former Africville resident

ers and students alike feared for their safety, the school was immediately closed. With much trepidation, the school reopened, hoping that the weight of tighter security and discipline would prevent further fighting. Some observers, however, argue that until the century-old tensions between the student's home-towns, North Preston, a predominantly black community, and Eastern Passage, a white settlement, are improved, Cole Harbour High will be at risk for further violence.

THE BLACK CULTURAL CENTRE

In 1972, Reverend Dr. William Pearly Oliver put forward a proposal to create a centre for cultural and educational programs to meet the needs and aspirations of the black communities of Nova Scotia. The Black Cultural Centre was the fruition of this proposal. Built on a three-acre lot just outside of Dartmouth, the centre opened its doors on September 17, 1983. It is operated by the Society for the Protection and Preservation of Black Culture in Nova Scotia (better know as the Black Cultural Society), which hosts a variety of cultural events across the province, including plays, concerts, workshops and lectures.

SURVEY SEZ: RACISM STILL FELT BY
BLACK STUDENTS IN NOVA SCOTIA

Even today, African Nova Scotians feel the sting of racism. In a 2003 survey, 23 percent of African Nova Scotian parents said their children had experienced racial discrimination at school.

They Said It

"If you pull one thing out to look at, then it seems quite simple, but when you begin to look below the surface you see how complicated that one issue is. And when you take several issues together, you have an intricate web that isn't easily pulled apart or fixed."
— **Parent of a Cole Harbour High student**

Take Five

In our fives chapter, what we wanted to give you was something you could literally count on one hand. It is designed to be fun, but at the same time revealing, both about our province, and the person making the choices. It is a chapter that could have continued well beyond the bounds of this book. Nova Scotians, famous and not so famous, were literally bursting at the seams with opinions about their province. This means, of course, we'll include more choices next time.

ASHLEY MACISAAC'S FIVE FAVOURITE NOVA SCOTIANS

When Ashley MacIsaac burst onto the world music scene in 1995 with his debut CD, "Hi, How Are You Today?" he became an overnight pop icon – the kilted rebel from Creignish. MacIsaac has heeded well his father's advice: "If you want to play the fiddle, get mad at it or don't play it at all." His energetic genius has stretched that instrument far beyond the traditional jigs and reels, weaving in such contemporary styles as punk, electronica, hip-hop and grunge.

1. **Alexander Graham Bell**. I am fascinated with him for his inventions, particularly his work with the deaf and blind girl Helen Keller. He was an amazing Scotsman/Cape Bretoner.

2. **Allan J. MacEachen**. This Deputy Prime Minister — from Cape Breton as well — served under Pierre Elliot Trudeau. When Trudeau was out of the country, he could lay claim to Acting Prime Minister. He also was health minister during the implementation of Canada's health care system. He is one of my biggest heroes.

3. **Rita MacNeil**. Through all adversity, this artist has proven that the power of music is something that can supercede image, financial background and stereotypes, not only in the music industry but in our country and around the world.

4. **Jerome Sullivan**. My English teacher in high school. He proved that with the right instruction and an adherence to fine literature and art, even little kids living in the woods can come to appreciate the finer things the creative world has to offer.

5. **Hank Snow**. A man who performed thousands of shows and songs recorded by such greats as Elvis Presley, Anne Murray and countless others, proves that even a small town boy from Nova Scotia can make it to the biggest stages in the world of show business.

MICHAEL HAYNES' FIVE FAVOURITE GREASY SPOONS

Why, you might ask, does Michael Haynes get two picks. As anybody who goes hiking or backpacking knows, after coming out of a few days of roughing it on the trail there is nothing better than chowing down to a heaping plate of fish and chips, or a big cheeseburger with all the trimmings. And who better to offer his list of the five best 'greasy spoons' than the consummate hiker himself, Michael Haynes. Haynes says every one of these restaurants has its 'best dish.' If you're looking for gourmet, go elsewhere, but if it's a good, satisfying feed you want, you can try one of these recommended food joints.

1. **Shillelagh House**, Truro (fish & chips)
2. **Turkey Burger**, New Germany (best names for burgers, home-made relishes)
3. **John's Lunch**, Dartmouth (clams & chips)
4. **Roadside Grill**, Belliveau Cove (really, really good clams and scallops)
5. **Irving Big Stop**, Auld's Cove (breakfast: bacon, eggs, home fries)

SUE MACLEOD'S FAVOURITE FICTIONAL CHARACTERS

Sue MacLeod is a poet who has published two collections of poetry, "The Language of Rain" and "That Singing You Hear at the Edges". MacLeod holds the distinction of being Halifax's first Poet Laureate, filling the post from 2001 to 2005. In this capacity she is the editor of an anthology of writing and photography, "To Find Us: Words and Images of Halifax". MacLeod grew up in Toronto, the daughter of a Cape Breton family, but now has spent most of her adult life in Halifax.

1. **Archibald.** I'll begin with the acknowledged master, Alistair MacLeod. Among my favourite of his characters is Archibald (full name only: "he did not look or act 'like an Archie,' as they said") in "The Tuning of Perfection." Archibald is one of "the last of the authentic old-time Gaelic singers," but he is far too real - too heartbreakingly real, when it comes down to it - to be mistaken for an artifact of folklore.

2. **Cù mòr glas.** Still on the subject of heartbreak, MacLeod's story "As Birds Bring Forth the Sun" has a canine character who "was never given a name but was referred to in Gaelic as cù mòr glas, the big grey dog." My first experience with this story was hearing MacLeod read it. When I look at the opening lines, his resonant voice comes back to me: "Once there was a family with a Highland name who lived by the sea. And the man had a dog of which he was very fond."

3. **Yuri** Maureen Hull's story, "Listening and Touching," features a character named Yuri. He's Russian, not Nova Scotian, but he used to shoot pool in a Halifax tavern that is easily recognizable as The Seahorse. Yuri stands out because of his sweet nature and a friendliness that bridges cultural gaps, though the narrator also likes him for his forearms, "pale and muscled," and "finely cut."

4. **Sal.** Another of Maureen Hull's characters is Sal, whose diary entries comprise the story, "Leap Year." Sal works at the Busy Bee Laundromat in a Nova Scotia town and reads the Reader's Digest's "It Pays to Enrich Your Word Power" column while she dreams of being someplace else. I like Sal for her wit, for her warmth, and for spicing up her entries with "vocabulary" words: "Since they cut back on her hours, she's as impecunious as the rest of us." Inimitable Sal.

5. **Miss Hancock.** And let's not forget Miss Hancock, the English teacher in Budge Wilson's "The Metaphor," a story of affection and betrayal. "Like a heavy bird, she fluttered and flitted from desk to desk," urging her students not to think too much, but to feel - and write - "without restraint, without inhibition, with verve." I like Miss Hancock because we all deserve at least one hopelessly enthusiastic English teacher. Hopefully, we treat her (or him) well.

JOEL PLASKETT'S FIVE FAVOURITE HALIFAX HANG-OUTS

Joel Plaskett was only 14 when he formed Thrush Hermit, the alternative rock band that grew from its suburban Clayton Park roots into a modest success in the vibrant Halifax indie pop-grunge explosion of the 1990s. Now 30 and playing both solo gigs and with his Joel Plaskett Emergency band, the lanky singer-songwriter-guitarist has a dozen recordings under his belt. And despite a 2003 reader's poll in The Coast newspaper that voted him one of the 'Most Likely Haligonians to Move to Toronto,' Plaskett says he's staying put. He's even immortalized his hometown in "Love this Town," a homage to Halifax recorded on his CD, "LaDeDa". This solo recording hit the top of the college music charts as soon as it was released in 2005, staying at number one for five straight weeks.

What does Plaskett like most about living in Halifax? "Its size and casualness. People are very supportive of my music here but they also tend to respect my privacy," he says.

1. **The Last Word Bookstore**, on Windsor Street in Halifax. "I like going here to talk about crime novels with the owner, Wayne."

2. **The Woodside Ferry Terminal parking lot**, towards Eastern Passage. "I like going here to eat take-out food while staring at the oil rigs."

3. **The Armview Restaurant** on Chebucto Rd at the rotary. "I like the rice pudding, the quiet, and watching cars go round in circles."

4. **Little Nashville**, on Wyse Road in Dartmouth. "This is like Nashville, only smaller."

5. **The Halifax-Dartmouth Ferry**. "Fifteen minutes to myself, and someone else is driving . . . a great way to start or end your day or night."

ANNE SIMPSON: FIVE PHRASES THAT DESCRIBE NOVA SCOTIA

What words would an award-winning poet use to describe Nova Scotia? This is the question we asked Anne Simpson of Antigonish. Her most recent collection of poems, "Loop", won the country's most prestigious poetry prize in 2004, the $40,000 Griffin Poetry Prize. She is also author of the novel, "Canterbury Beach", and another book of poetry, Light Falls Through You, winner of the Atlantic Poetry Prize. Simpson has lived in France and in Italy and worked for two years as a teacher in Nigeria before moving to Nova Scotia about 15 years ago. Today she teaches part-time at St. Francis Xavier

University, where she also co-ordinates the Great Blue Heron Writing Workshop. In 2005-2006 she is also the writer-in-residence for the Pictou Antigonish Regional Library.

1. a glide of eagles over Monk's Head
2. yellow-gold leaves – an old tree, wakened
3. threaded through snow, a whisky-coloured stream
4. now the dancers: five deer
5. home, the scent of bread

ECOLOGY ACTION CENTER'S FIVE TOP ENVIRONMENTAL ACHIEVEMENTS

Who would have thought that a group formed out of a 1971 Dalhousie University "Ecology and Action" class would go on to become the region's largest and most active environmental organization. After almost 35 years in operation, Nova Scotia's Ecology Action Centre has a membership of more than 700, a volunteer force of over 200, seven active issues committees and a dozen or so people on staff. Over the years they have fought to protect endangered species, wilderness areas, deep sea corals and pedestrian-friendly cities. The staff at EAC have collectively come up with a list of what they consider to be Nova Scotia's top five environmental achievements:

1. **The Gully Marine Protection Area**. The Gully was the first Marine Protected Area in Atlantic Canada. It lies off the coast of Nova Scotia and is home to a vast number of marine species, from corals to whales.

2. **Nova Scotia's Wilderness Protection Act**. Since its enactment in 1998, the Wilderness Protection Act has secured over 33 protected areas, including the most recent acquisitions of Gully Lake and Eigg Mountain.

3. **Pesticide By-law**. HRM adopted Nova Scotia's first pesticide by-law and has since prevented the usage of gallons of harmful chemicals. Pesticide by-laws are now becoming major issues in other Nova Scotian municipalities.

4. **The Nova Scotia Recycling Program**. Starting in the early seventies as a group of volunteers collecting paper in Halifax, the Nova Scotia recycling program has grown province-wide and is now one of the best programs for recycling in North America.

5. **Support for local and organic foods**. The increasing successes of Nova Scotia's many farmer's markets is a strong indication of the mounting interest in buying local and environmentally-friendly foods. Farmer's markets are now all over Nova Scotia, including North America's longest running farmer's market in Halifax.

TIM TREGUNNO'S FIVE HARDIEST NOVA SCOTIA FLOWERS

Tim Tregunno is the president and general manager of Halifax Seed. He is third generation owner of the oldest operating seed company in Canada (established in 1866). A lifelong resident of Nova Scotia (excluding a short stint during university days in New Brunswick), he has been involved in the business since 1979 on a full-time basis, and for many other years as summer employment.

1. **Lupin**
2. **Daylily**
3. **Petunia**
4. **Black-Eyed Susan**
5. **Shasta Daisy**

HARV STEWART'S TOP FIVE CURRENT SPORTING FIGURES

Harv Stewart has been sports director and a morning show co-host at Q-104 Radio since 1990. He is also the of host Eastlink's Harv's Sportsland. Prior to coming to *Nova Scotia, he worked in Alberta covering the Oilers, Eskimos, Flames, Stamps and the 1988 Winter Games. He now calls Nova Scotia and Halifax his full-time home.*

1. **Sidney Crosby**. At age 18, has dominated every hockey league he's played in and is now going to the NHL. He has the same characteristics – poise, humility and grit – of other greats like Howe, Gretzky and Lemieux. He is now being asked to help resurrect the NHL, a league that's been decimated by labour trouble. He is currently one of our most famous Canadians, and still a teenager!

2. **Colleen Jones**. Could be listed as the best curler ever, male or female. Her résumé of World and Canadian women's titles tells the story. She has only gotten better with age.

3. **Al MacInnis**. The pride of Port Hood – one of the best NHL defensemen ever to play the game. He has won the Stanley Cup in Calgary, the Norris Trophy, and an Olympic gold medal. He is the complete package. He came up as the hardest shooter in the league, but then refined his other skills to become a team leader and future Hall of Famer.

4. **Steve Konchalski**. Has been the head basketball coach at St. F.X. University for more than thirty years. He has led the X-men to several national titles and was also the Canadian senior men's coach. His recruiting and teaching success are legendary.

5. **Don Koharski**. The Dartmouth native is the one you're not supposed to notice – the NHL official. But in the NHL, he is the man the league uses as referee in crucial games. He has appeared in more than ten Stanley Cup finals.

TRUDY FONG'S FIVE FAVOURITE
NOVA SCOTIA BACKROADS

Trudy Fong knows all about getting off the beaten track. Once, on a three-year journey around the world, she got herself sidetracked in Hong Kong and spent over a year working for the daily newspaper, The Hong Kong Standard. She did finally make her way back home to Nova Scotia, where she continues to write about travel, among other things, from her home in Dartmouth. Fong is the author of the popular Insiders' Guide: "Off the Beaten Path", Maritime Provinces, which is now in its fifth edition.

1. **Antigonish to Jeddore along Highway 7**. The portion of the Marine Drive, which follows Route 7 from exit 32 outside Antigonish until you reach Jeddore, presents a time traveller's picture of the Atlantic Coast. You can make a complete family vacation out of a tiny bit of geography, enjoying along the way some excellent nature, including eagles' nests and a salmon ladder. Liscombe Lodge offers some nice accommodations, including cabins overlooking the rapids of the St. Mary's River. Nearby is the excellent 'living history' site of Sherbrooke Village, which features a collection of houses dating back to the village's 1860s Gold Rush. Further up the road is Taylor Head beach followed by the famous salmon smokehouse, Willy Krauch and Sons in Tangier.

2. **Digby Neck, Long Island and Briar Island**. This whole area is really part of the Bay of Fundy's long trail of prehistoric lava that runs along the coastline. It's also a prime location for whale and dolphin sightings and many species of migratory birds. Follow Route 217 from Digby until you reach a small car ferry to Long Island. There are many glorious igneous rock formations along this coastline, which resembles Western Ireland. Finally, take the ferry to Briar Island where you can join a whale cruise or hike out to Green Head to admire the view: the towering basalt cliffs of Peter's Island are home to a bird sanctuary inhabited in the summer by thousands of Arctic Terns.

3. **The Cabot Trail, or Route 19**, which skirts the northern perimeter of Cape Breton Highlands National Park. Of course that means you get to start in the heartland of Nova Scotia's most musical region, next enjoy the vibrant village of Cheticamp, and then drive through forests of 300-year-old sugar maples, yellow birch and beech trees. On a clear day you can see the Magdalene Islands. The park features 28 suggested hiking trails and at the tail end of your Cabot Trail voyage, there are several good accommodation options if you want to stay longer.

4. **Liverpool to Shelburne**. From historic Liverpool south along Highway 103/Route 3 until Shelburne you can have a complete vacation in the palm of your hand. First you have the wilderness offered by the Kejimkujik Seaside Adjunct and Pocket Wilderness areas. Then you can follow Route 3 into the pretty village of Lockeport, site of the province's first officially designated heritage streetscape. Right alongside the entrance to the town is Crescent Beach, one of the province's finest, and as warm as you are going to get on the Atlantic Coastline. You can cap your holiday off with a visit to Shelburne, where thousands of United Empire Loyalists once made it the third largest town in North America. The downtown was rebuilt for use in the filming of *The Scarlet Letter* with Demi Moore.

5. **Glooscap Trail**. Skirting the shores of the Minas Basin any time of the year is a scenic delight. From Windsor, leave Highway 101 at Exit 5 and follow Route 215 along the Glooscap Trail. Here the world's highest tides reach their peak at Burntcoat Head. Nearby you can join one of several tour operations for a river rafting adventure that rides these high tides up the Shubenacadie River. You can continue your trip along the Glooscap Trail via Portapique, featuring the home and studio of painter Joy Laking, then the Dominion Chair Company in Bass River, and finally camp out at the wonder-

ful Five Island Provincial Park near Economy. This area is a mecca for geology buffs, and in the pleasant town of Parrsboro you can find some civilized pursuits as well, such as joining a rock hounding or fossil tour with the Fundy Geological Museum.

BRUCE NUNN'S FIVE SURPRISING
NOVA SCOTIAN CONNECTIONS TO THE WORLD

Bruce Nunn knows how to tell a story. As Mr. Nova Scotia Know-It-All, he has been regaling CBC Radio listeners for almost a decade with regular doses of twisted but factual tales of obscure Maritime history. A graduate of Saint Francis Xavier University in Antigonish, Nunn is the author of three books of stories: History with a Twist, More History with a Twist and, more recently, 59 Stories: Nova Scotia's Curious Connections to the Remarkable, the World-Famous and the Strange. He's also written two children's Christmas books, The Magical Christmas Light of Old Nova Scotia and Buddy, the Bluenose Reindeer.

1. A **Duke Ellington** jazz ballad I discovered in 1998 entitled Clara was named – just as Duke had promised her – for a Halifax woman, Clara Carvery Adams, a cousin of Duke's 1930s lover, Mildred Dixon, whose family came from Halifax's Africville.

2. In the very first **Superman comic book**, issued in 1939, the storyline was borrowed from Nova Scotia's infamous 1936 Moose River Gold Mine collapse. In the comic, Superman helps the 'draegermen,' a word the Oxford Canadian Dictionary says was coined in Nova Scotia, citing as evidence its use at the Moose River (Halifax County) mine rescue.

3. **Alexander Graham Bell** was just one of several who convinced inventor Guiglielmo Marconi to move his work from Newfoundland to Cape Breton, where Marconi set up the world's first trans-oceanic wireless messaging service.

4. Nova Scotian **Abraham Gesner** launched today's petroleum industry by inventing a new fuel he called 'kerosene,' first tested as a new lighthouse fuel (replacing whale oil) at the lighthouse on the beach of McNab's Island in Halifax harbour.

5. **Archibald MacMechan**, a literature professor at Dalhousie University in Halifax at the turn of the 20th century, championed Herman Melville's little known 1851 novel to literary contacts and the general public so successfully that Moby Dick became the household word and the literary classic it is today.

NANCY STEVENS' FIVE FAVORITE LANDSCAPES

The Nova Scotia landscape has been an inspiration for painters for centuries. Noted among them is Nancy Stevens, a Fine Arts graduate of Mount Allison University who has taught landscape painting at NSCAD and St. F.X. University. Although her current interests are on large acrylic abstracts, Stevens continues to be drawn to the elements of shape and colour found in Nova Scotia's countryside and coastlines. We asked Nancy Stevens to describe her five favourite places to paint.

1. **Martinique Beach**. This location always provides inspiration: the pinks and purples of the rocks and the surprisingly turquoise water; at other times the division of space on the paper of a dramatic sky and sea or the textures of a foreground of pebbles and beach grasses.

2. **Annapolis Valley**. Several Annapolis Valley apple orchards have been my subject matter, especially in spring when in blossom and in late summer laden with ripe fruit. The regular pattern of trees, the rounded forms of distant hills and a meandering Avon river have wonderful design possibilities.

3. **Antigonish Harbour**. I always marvel at the ever-changing Antigonish Harbour, fields in foreground and forested hills on oppo-

site shore. I have painted this landscape in winter when the harbour has been frozen, the land snow-covered, dark conifers patterning the whiteness; and in autumn when the colours were glowing and warm, the atmosphere soft and the water reflected a hazy light.

4. **Yarmouth County**. Painting the coast of Yarmouth County often presents a challenge because of the moisture in the air. When I painted the graceful arc of the beach at Port Maitland, the colours were muted and I tried to capture a quality of light that blurred the horizon and made the opalescent colours of wet and dry sand and shallow water dance and shimmer.

5. **Lake Ainslie**. Using both watercolours and acrylics to paint the hills surrounding Lake Ainslie, I have often been intimidated by the drama of that landscape. Vignettes of fields of goldenrod and late summer grasses sloping down to the lake accented by dark spruce, and a group of trees where eagles nest high on a hill overlooking the lake, have been more successful than the big scene.

MARJORIE WILLISON'S FIVE FAVOURITE EDIBLE PLANTS

You won't find a greener thumb in Nova Scotia than that of Marjorie Willison. Willison picked up her love of plants as a child, helping out in the family gardens in Alberta. Since moving to Nova Scotia in the early 1970s, she has thrown herself into the world of gardening. Today the popular columnist, author and phone-in guest applies that know-how to assist and encourage gardeners around the Maritimes to grow their own foods and flowers. Her books include "Easy Garden Planning" and "The Complete Gardener's Almanac: a month by month guide to gardening year round".

Willison says it was easy to choose her five favourite plants — they are all edible. She says the plants give her great pleasure because she and her husband nurture them together. She says she delights in the feeling of self-reliance that comes from growing at least some of their own food.

1. **Indian Pear.** My favourite small tree has many names – Indian Pear, Juneberry, Shadblow, Serviceberry, and Amelanchier. I love its clouds of creamy white flowers in spring, and the rich, rust colour of its leaves in autumn. The dark summer berries add colour and flavour to fruit dishes of all kinds, and its multiple stems make a superb windbreak in winter.

2. **Raspberry.** The ubiquitous raspberry is my favourite cane fruit. Forest soil in Nova Scotia, exposed to sunlight after many years of shade, will produce raspberry plants from seeds long hidden in the soil. Just remember to cut out the old canes each year, and keep the clumps of canes thinned far enough apart that a dog could run through the patch.

3. **Potato.** Perhaps it is the Irish in me, but my favourite source of carbohydrates is the humble potato. Varieties developed in other parts of the world seem to thrive in Nova Scotia, perhaps because of our cool summers and damp soils. Whether you like them baked, boiled, mashed, scalloped, broiled, added to hodgepodge or turned into salad, potatoes nourish the body and comfort the soul.

4. **Tomatoe.** I can hardly wait each year for my first taste of garden-fresh tomatoes, my favourite annual vegetable. My favourite way of eating sliced, fresh tomatoes is covered with pieces of goat cheese, dressed with balsamic vinegar, olive oil, and a little salt, then garnished with snippets of fresh basil. Extra tomatoes are turned into a variety of soups and sauces, and also canned, frozen or dried. When frosty autumn days arrive, maturing tomatoes ripen slowly indoors, and green tomatoes are transformed into rich mincemeat for winter feasting.

5. **Asparagus.** My favourite perennial vegetable is marvelous asparagus, which comes up every spring in delectable spears without me having to plant it each year. A well-cared-for asparagus bed will produce for many years. Each spring, spread a one-inch layer of compost or manure over the bed, and another layer after harvest is complete. Through the summer, keep every blade of grass and sprig of weed out of the bed to reduce competition for moisture and nutrients, and remove old fronds every autumn. Then sit back in winter and dream about the first taste of asparagus and all those other delicious garden plants next season.

COLLEEN JONES' FIVE FAVOURITE SPORTING ACTIVITIES

As a five-time winner of the Canadian Women's Curling Championship and two-time World Curling champ, Colleen Jones knows something about sports. Jones has been in the public eye since she won the first of 16 Nova Scotia curling titles for Halifax's Mayflower Curling Club when she was only 19 years old. Although she's considered the most successful Canadian women's skip in curling history, Jones doesn't confine her sporting activities to just curling. The woman who knows how to balance two careers and the demands of raising a family also knows how to enjoy her free time.

1. **Biking**. If you love to bike, the bike ride from Chester to Lunenburg on the old road (Highway 3) is fabulous—the hills aren't too painful. You start with a chocolate milkshake at the Windjammer for extra energy and you're set. It's been years since I've done the ride ... but the beauty is something that stays with you forever.

2. **Golfing**. I hate to golf, but I love to golf in Inverness at Highland Links. While my golf game is brutal, it's a fabulous walk with great views and apparently one of the best golf courses in Canada—which sort of goes over my head considering my game.

3. **Running**. While you'd have to travel many times around the world to find as great a running locale as Point Pleasant Park, I prefer the Frog Pond, on the Purcell's Cove Road. While I have yet to see one frog, you see plenty of ducks and the odd beaver building their dams. It's an easy run, with beautiful lake views on wooded paths … a bit of paradise in the city.

4. **Rowing**. One of the oldest rowing clubs in North America is the Halifax Rowing Club on the Northwest Arm. I took lessons with my friend Linda Alexander—and while we had dreams of competing in the Olympics, we had to settle for lots of Zen-like experiences at sixa.m. on flat water watching the sun rise over McNabb's Island.

5. **Swimming**. This one will always be heavily debated in the province, because some people love Liverpool, others Northumberland Strait, and others are Lawrencetown Beach bums . . . but for great sand, privacy and reasonably warm water, Bachman's Island in Mahone Bay is wonderful. Of course you need a boat to get there–a minor detail–but well worth the trip for swimming at your own private island!

ALLAN LYNCH'S FIVE FAVOURITE PLACES
Allan Lynch is one of Nova Scotia's best and most prolific travel writers. His work has appeared in magazines and journals across North America and Europe. He brings with him wit and insight, the result of a lifetime spent traveling. As he puts it, trying to narrow down a list to five favourite places is tough because Nova Scotia is so deliciously diverse and eccentric.

1. **Annapolis Royal/Port Royal**. This is such a pretty, quiet area, it's hard to realize it's one of the most fought-over places in Canada. I also love the idea that this is home to the first permanent European settlement in Canada . . . that this is where the nation began. Few countries can claim to so definitively know their roots.

2. **Baddeck**. It's easy to understand why the beauty of this place so inspired Alexander Graham Bell. I also like the ability to cruise on the lake or visit the Gaelic College in nearby St. Ann's. One of the highlights for me is learning about Bell, the man, at the Alexander Graham Bell National Historic Site. His inventions are stunning, but the video memories of estate workers and his daughters are the real highlight of the museum.

3. **Lunenburg**. This is like some sort of fantastical architectural playground, with brightly coloured, overly decorated buildings. The streets are full of wonderfully pokey little shops and their calendar is stuffed with cool events from the Folk Art Festival, Folk Harbour Festival, and summer and Christmas crafts markets. The air also seems fresher here.

4. **The dykes behind Wolfville**. This is part of the legacy of the Acadians who were deported in 1755. Their ingenuity and back-breaking labour reclaimed thousands of acres from the sea. Four hundreds years later, the dykes are still doing their job, only now they provide a great place to walk and bike. In two minutes you can go from pavement to watching herons, harbour porpoise and seabirds.

5. **Our museums**. Nova Scotia is the pack-rat province. With more than 250 museums, we've shown our inability to throw anything away. The result is a truly fabulous collection of national historic sites as well as provincial and local museums. I like that the Nova Scotia Museum complex covers not just the grand mansions of the elite, like Uniacke House, but also preserves lives of the modest people who built this province, illustrated by places like the Fisherman's Life Museum (Jeddore). I find the Museum of Industry (Stellarton), J.C. Williams Dory Shop (Shelburne) and the Margaree Salmon Museum more fascinating than I thought they could be. I like the grandeur of Louisbourg, the sacred quiet of Grand Pré National Historic Site, and

the stunning views from the Highland Village in Iona.

Yarmouth's Firefighter's Museum is a hoot and taught me about early firefighting ingenuity, while the Glace Bay Miners' Museum will frighten any kid into getting a first-class education. Sherbrooke Village looks so pretty it's hard to believe it's real. The William deGarthe Gallery (Peggy's Cove) shows work that is well beyond the well-known Christmas card images, as well as the romantic story surrounding his last painting. Then there are the small gems, like the North Hills Museum (on the road to Port Royal) and Prescott House (Star's Point).

We can do worse in this province than getting out to rediscover who we are and who helped us get where we are. Our museums have an inspiring story to tell.

MURIEL DUCKWORTH'S FIVE INSPIRATIONAL NOVA SCOTIA WOMEN

Muriel Duckworth's name has been synonymous with the peace movement in Nova Scotia for decades. Duckworth is a founding member of the group, Voice of Women for Peace, and is one of nine Canadian women included in the 1000 Women for the Nobel Peace Prize 2005 nomination. She is now in her mid-nineties. For her five favourites, Duckworth has chosen five women – four singer/songwriters and a filmmaker – "from the large number of Nova Scotia artists who have inspired me with the vision they have for the world."

1. **Andrea Currie**. Member of the former singing group Four the Moment. Andrea and her guitar and I travelled together to a gathering in Sherbrooke a long time ago. She played her instrument and had everyone singing.

2. **Cheryl Gaudet**. Says she was inspired to write her song, "Feed the People," when she sang at the Women's International Conference for Peace held at Mount Saint Vincent University in 1985. "Feed the people; house the children/ Ask the questions; find

solutions/ Stop producing ammunition/ Form a world-wide coalition/ Why not do it right instead of wrong?"

3. **Sandy Greenberg**. I think I first met Sandy when she was involved in the Peaceful Schools movement. Sandy has created a song for the peace movement. It begins,
"This is a song for our mother the earth.
 This is a song for all our children.
 We will study war no more.
 It's time to study peace."

4. **Sylvia Hamilton**: I went to the opening of Sylvia Hamilton's film Black Mother, Black Daughter and there wasn't enough room in the hall for everyone who wanted to see it. I have found her a great stimulation for me.

5. **Rose Vaughan**. My favourite creation of Rose Vaughan's is her very soothing song, "Stone and sand and sea and fog." With all the turmoil and tragedy, greed and destruction around us, I find this song has a spiritual message about all creation, and a serenity which is important to me.

ALAIN MEUSE'S FIVE FAVOURITE FISH STORIES
Alain Meuse has been editor of "The Sou'wester", the commercial fishing newspaper of record in Canada for the Atlantic coast, for more than 30 years. From his perch in Yarmouth, he has witnessed the booms and the collapses of the most dangerous, volatile, and important industry in the province. He has also born witness to government double talk and tall tales, and he has relayed those to his readers for almost forty years.

1. **Bluefin Blue**. We were on a bus traveling back to Toronto from the RMC College in Kingston, Ontario, way back in the early 60s where our squad, the Ryerson Rams football team, had demol-

ished the soon-to-be military geniuses 60 to nil when the talk turned to fishing.

One fellow from Northern Ontario kept bragging about the three-foot northern pikes he caught the previous summer.

"Hey, Bluenose. What's the biggest fish you ever caught?" he queried moi.

"Well, not that many. Only went eeling when I was a kid. But I was on a boat once where an eight or nine incher was hauled in. Took the guy six and a half hours," I replied.

Guffaws all around.

"Eight or nine inch? Eight or nine inch what, minnow?" he charged.

More hee haws.

"Oh. Forgot to add that down east we measure 'em between the eyes, bys. The eyes."

Name was Bluefin Blue from then on . . . .

2. **Quiet Canadian**. It was early June and the water was low on the Barios when I decided to take my friend Hayden for some brook trout fishing.

By that time fly fishing was the rigueur on that river but Hayden was and is a die-hard metal caster.

They just weren't biting that day and to top it off Hayden kept losing lures to a weedy bottom and rocks festooned with green algae.

He looked a bit puzzled as he scratched around his lure box. He finally told me he was down to his last lure. I looked as he tied on a greenish bunch of fur and tassel on his line.

Lord, I thought. Green thing-a-ma-jig with all that green stuff in the water? No chance in hell. But you don't correct a friend. Never.

I watched in amazement as on just his second cast he pulled in a pound-and-a-halfer.

We left shortly after. After all, I was driving. Was a quiet ride back, as I remember. From my side anyway.

3. **Beaver**. My friend Bucky was fishing the Annis River one late summer evening when he tied into a monster 'salmon.' Try as he may he couldn't angle the thing close to the net. It came in, then stripped his line so hard and fast that his fly fishing reel began to complain.

Now Becky is a world class angler but even he couldn't figure out this one. And the night was closing in fast.

When the 'salmon' started to head out to the lake that empties into the river, Bucky knew the gig was up, in a way.

Then a peculiar thing happened; his 'salmon' climbed onto a rock!

He had hooked Canada's national symbol, the noble and ingenious beaver!

"It was a tough wade but I got my fly back anyway. He wasn't too pleased when I yanked the hook out of his fur but a good fly is a good fly," he said.

4. **Legend of Sneezy Mac**. I won't name the person to protect the guilty.

He was trouting with a pair of friends one lazy summer afternoon. Well, they were fishing, he wasn't, tending a stash of cool Oland's Export Ale.

But the boys couldn't land anything; hooked aplenty but nothing aboard the canoe.

"Give me the damn rod," he bellowed.

One was handed to him.

He took a piece of wool from his sleeveless shirt and some hair from his nostrils and asked one of the pair to tie his opus on the hook, which they obliged amidst giggles which almost tipped the canoe.

Lo and behold the fly worked like a charm.

We named it Sneezy Mac on the spot.

5. **Let Their Be Light**. We were in camp one evening and over cards and 'coffee' the talk turned to big fish.

"Caught an eight pound brookie down by the Little Meadow last spring," a newcomer to the gang muttered.

We all looked at him.

No such thing as an eight pound brookie. Only in dreams.

"Well," drawled, one of the ole buddies. "Was jigging for cod out by Jacko last summer and what did I haul up but a ten pound cod with a hurricane lantern wrapped around his lips. And it was lit!"

After the laughter subsided, the newcomer dared to question the fact of the lit lantern.

"Impossible!" he growled.

"OK," said the old buddy. "You take five pounds off your trout and I'll blow out the lantern!"

Amen . . .